馬

THE DIARY OF MA YAN

燕

日

記

Ma Yan in

THE DIARY OF
Ma Yan

馬燕日記

The Struggles and Hopes of
a Chinese Schoolgirl

Edited and introduced by Pierre Haski

Translated from the French by Lisa Appignanesi

The diaries were originally translated from
the Mandarin by He Yanping

HARPERCOLLINSPUBLISHERS

Library of Congress Cataloging-in-Publication Data
Ma, Yan, 1987–
    The diary of Ma Yan : the struggles and hopes of a Chinese schoolgirl / Ma Yan ; edited and introduced by Pierre Haski ; translated from the French by Lisa Appignanesi.—1st American ed.
        p.   cm.
    "The diaries were originally translated from the Mandarin by He Yanping."
    "Originally published in France by Editions Ramsay, 2002."
    Audience: Ages 10–up.
    Audience: Grades 5–up.
    ISBN 0-06-076496-1 — ISBN 0-06-076497-X (lib. bdg.)
    1. Ma, Yan, 1987–—Diaries—Juvenile literature. 2. Girls—China—Diaries—Juvenile literature. I. Title: Struggles and hopes of a Chinese school-girl. II. Haski, Pierre. III. Title.
CT1828.M34A3 2005   2004016136
951.05'9'08352—dc22   CIP
                                                                          AC

Typography by Sasha Illingworth
1 2 3 4 5 6 7 8 9 10
❖
First American Edition, 2005
Originally published in France by Éditions Ramsay, 2002
The photos on pages 63, 67, 96, 106, and 142 are by Wang Zheng.
The photos on pages ii, 4, 16, 22, 30, 43, 50, 78, 98, 112, 116, 123, 134, 158, 163, and 167 are by Pierre Haski.
The photos on pages viii, 10, and 90 are by Vincent Angouillant.

ACKNOWLEDGMENTS

Our sincerest thanks go to translator He Yanping, who has also been engaged in aid work for the children of the Ningxia region; to the photographer, Wang Zheng, who was our guide; to Sarah Neiger, who was instrumental in setting up this adventure; and to all those, both in China and Europe, who have supported Ma Yan and the children of Ningxia.

CONTENTS

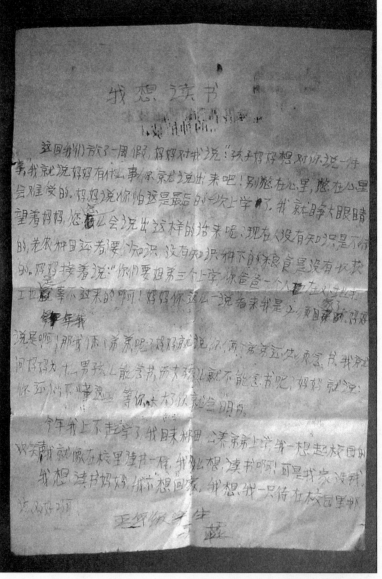

Ma Yan's letter, translated on the facing page

I WANT TO STUDY

We have a week of vacation. Mother takes me aside.

"My child. There's something I have to tell you."

I answer, "Mother, if you have something to tell me, do it quickly. Tell me."

But her words are like a death sentence.

"I'm afraid you may have been to school for the last time."

My eyes go wide. I look up at her. "How can you say something like that? These days you can't live without an education. Even a peasant needs knowledge to ensure good harvests and to farm well."

Mother insists. "Your brothers and you add up to three children to be sent to school. Your father is the only one earning money, and it's not enough."

I'm frightened. "Does this mean I have to come home to work?"

"Yes."

"And my two brothers?"

"Your two brothers will carry on with their studies."

I protest. "Why can boys study and not girls?"

Her smile is tired. "You're still little. When you grow up, you'll understand."

1

No more money for school this year. I'm back in the house and I work the land in order to pay for my brothers' education. When I think of the happy times at school, I can almost imagine myself there. How I want to study! But my family can't afford it.

I want to go to school, Mother. I don't want to work at home. How wonderful it would be if I could stay at school forever!

Ma Yan
May 2, 2001

HOW IT HAPPENED

May 2001

The village of Zhangjiashu is a little like the end of the world; you don't come upon it by accident. Travel to Zhangjiashu, located thousands of miles northwest of China's capital, Beijing, is as much a journey through time as it is through space. Houses are built of brick and roofed with traditional tiles, and the village, spread unevenly along the hills, occupies a space far removed from the bubbling modernization of urban China. The village's inhabitants were amazed that we had taken less than twenty-four hours to get there from Beijing. For them, the capital is light years away.

In this remote corner of China, children are unaccustomed to seeing strangers. An official had told me that I was the first foreign journalist to come to the region since the 1930s. The very sight of our small journalistic crew had created unusual excitement. Now, having reached the end of our visit, we were getting ready to leave. The road before us was long and difficult, and our driver was impatient to start.

At that moment a village woman wearing the white head covering of the Chinese Muslims approached us. She held a letter and three small brown notebooks covered in finely drawn

The barren landscape around the village of Zhangjiashu

Chinese characters. She insisted, as if her very life depended on it, that we take them. We left a few minutes later, carrying this mysterious and apparently precious bundle with us.

A translation of just a little of what we had been given revealed a startling text, as well as the identity of its author. She was Ma Yan, then a girl of thirteen, in the midst of a crisis. In the letter, addressed to her mother—the very woman who had given us the notebooks—Ma Yan shouts a protest. She has just learned that she won't be able to go back to school. After five consecutive years of drought, her family no longer has the money to pay her school fees.

"I want to study," Ma Yan exclaims in the headline of the letter, written on the back of a seed packet for green beans. The letter had been scribbled in anger, as the various tears in the paper show. To pay for the ballpoint pen she used, we later learned, she had deprived herself of food for fifteen days.

The three little brown notebooks that came to us with Ma Yan's letter contained her personal diary. These pages gave us an intimate sense of the everyday life of a teenager whose life mirrors that of millions of others in the Chinese countryside. Many share her passionate desire for the education that will allow her and her family to escape poverty; many are tormented, like her, by the anxiety that they won't make the grade; many struggle against constant hunger and the sometimes harsh human relationships that can be part of an impoverished life.

Page by page, Ma Yan shows an increasing command both of her writing and of her feelings. Her first days as a schoolgirl in 2000, when she is thirteen, are the subject of the briefest, most understated notes. Then, before our eyes, Ma Yan gains in stature. Her life is a tough and fast teacher.

A month after our first visit, we decided to return to Zhangjiashu to meet Ma Yan and her mother.

We discovered that Ma Yan had returned to school. Her mother understood her distress and made the sacrifice of going off to do hard labor two hundred and fifty miles away to earn money for Ma Yan's education.

When we finally met Ma Yan, we found a girl with short hair and a lot of character. She was simply dressed in a white shirt and red canvas trousers. Around her neck there was a small plastic

heart on a chain, and she sported two silver-plated hoops in her ears. Lively and intelligent, she beamed at us, so very happy to have taken up her school life again. She didn't hide her joy when she learned that we'd come because of her.

Without any sign of being intimidated, Ma Yan told us her story, recounting her great sadness when she thought she might never be able to return to school. She talked about the gratitude she owed her mother and about the hopes her family had vested in her, their eldest child. Her sense of duty to her family was linked with defiance. If she can only get far enough with her studies, she'll be the first to escape from the dual burden of a harsh, desert soil and a strictly traditional society. She was fired up by the challenge.

Bai Juhua, Ma Yan's mother, joined us. Her features were drawn. A white head scarf covered her long black hair. She looked at her daughter tenderly, and it's clear that the two are very close. Tears streamed down her weary face. Her emotion was audible in her voice. "I'm a mother, but my heart was heavy. I knew that I couldn't send my daughter back to school. Ma Yan gave me her letter, but I can't read. She insisted, 'Read it and you'll know how unhappy I am.' I had it read to me and I understood."

Ma Yan's mother is only thirty-three, but years of hard work have made her look twenty years older. She has had no education, she can neither read nor write, but she knows that her daughter's salvation—like that of the rest of her family—depends on her being educated. On several occasions, she has taken Ma Yan out of school because she could not afford the fees. But at

6

each point Ma Yan struggled to continue. This girl is stubborn, her father claims proudly.

Ma Yan is unusual in this village, where most of the girls never have more than three or four years of schooling, barely time enough to learn to read and write. Ma Yan is now in her seventh year.

"Others stop much sooner," Ma Yan said sweetly. "I can only praise my parents."

During our visit to Zhangjiashu, a Chinese friend, who had accompanied us from the regional capital, predicted a bleak future for Ma Yan. Adversity and the weight of tradition would bring the girl down, as they had done others in the village, he told us.

"A family as poor as hers can't afford to pay for their daughter's education. She'll be engaged at sixteen, because her family needs the money her marriage will bring in to pay for their younger sons' marriages. The boys will take precedence." (In China, a man must make a gift of money to the family of his bride-to-be.) "Ma Yan is intelligent, but she can't escape that fate. It's her unalterable destiny."

But Ma Yan's mother denied this categorically. "I'll fight to my last breath so that my daughter doesn't have the same life as I had."

When mother and daughter embrace, there's more at stake than just strong emotion. The energy that flows between them is that of two women prepared to confront and challenge fate.

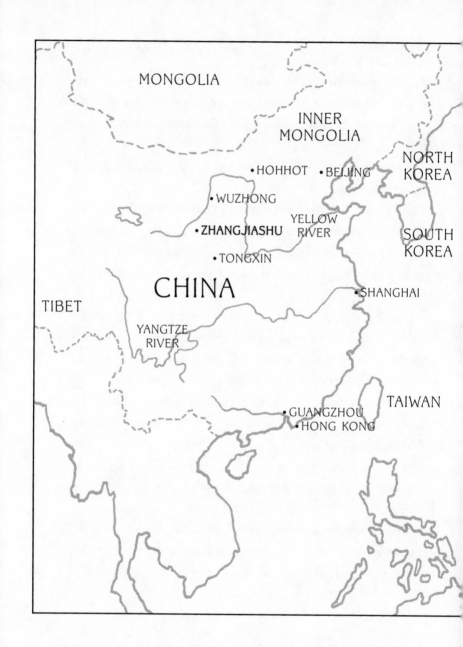

A NOTE ON NAMES AND CURRENCY

In China it is customary to list last names first. *Ma* is Ma Yan's family name. It is also a common surname in this area of China, and although many of Ma Yan's friends have the same family name, most are not related to her. Women in China do not change their names when they marry, so while Ma Yan's father and brothers are named Ma Dongji, Ma Yichao, and Ma Yiting, her mother is known by her maiden name, Bai Juhua.

Ma Yan and the people around her frequently refer to one another as *comrade*, a term that became popular during the Chinese Revolution of the 1940s.

The main Chinese currencies Ma Yan refers to are the fen and the yuan. One hundred fen equals one yuan. In American currency, one yuan is worth approximately twelve cents.

Pages from Ma Yan's d

THE DIARY: PART ONE

The diaries of Ma Yan are divided into two parts. The first part runs from September 2 to December 28, 2000; the second from July 3 to December 13, 2001. The breaks are due to lost notebooks. The sections of this book that explain details of Ma Yan's daily life were written by Pierre Haski.

Ma Yan started school at age eight, one year after most other pupils. Until then she had helped her mother with domestic chores and in the fields. Her first four school years were spent at the elementary school in Zhangjiashu. For her fifth year she went to middle school in Yuwang, a market town twelve and a half miles away from her home. At the time the diary starts, she's living at the Yuwang school during the week and traveling home for the weekends. Her brother Ma Yichao is in the same class as Ma Yan.

When she wrote her first entry, Ma Yan was thirteen and in her last year of elementary school. Her diary stops when she is in the first year of middle school and fourteen years old.

Just like every morning, I wash my face then brush my teeth. Soon the bell rings, marking the beginning of classes. A teacher arrives. He's wearing a blue jacket and black trousers and he has black leather shoes. He explains what he expects of us. I think he's our Chinese teacher.

A second teacher comes in. He tells us never to take things that belong to others and to think very carefully about what we say. Then he starts the lesson and gives us exercises to do. We do the work he's asked of us until class is over.

We go off to eat. Bai Xiaohua, in class three of the fifth year, brings in a pail full of water. We wash our faces and hands and then clean the dormitory. Bai Xiaohua sprinkles water on the floor. Yang Haiyan shakes out the beds. Ma Yuehua and I sweep the floor. Ma Juan has gone out—I don't know where—instead of helping us. Having done the cleaning, we sit down to rest for a bit, until the bell rings again.

Sunday, September 3
A fine day

This morning while I was busy working in class, my father and mother came to visit. They came to Yuwang for the fair. Before going back to it, they said to me, "You must work hard in order to get into the high school for girls." Then they went.

This afternoon a teacher showed us some gymnastics. If we can't do them, we have to get out of line and sing or dance. Then we have to start again, until we've managed to get through all the exercises. A few comrades, both boys and girls, finally managed it all, and the teacher congratulated them: "Those who've succeeded can go back to class."

Finally we all got through and went back to our classrooms.

This afternoon the music teacher, a twenty-year-old woman with a braid over three feet long, taught us the "Song of the Long March." She is our only woman teacher. First she sings with us a few times, then she lets us sing in chorus. Then she chooses one of us to sing alone, and another to dance in accompaniment. Everyone gets a turn, row by row. We've only reached the third row when the bell rings.

Wednesday, September 6
A gray day

This afternoon our Chinese teacher gave us an exercise to copy into our notebook. Two boys fought over a pencil,* as often happens. Before we even realized what had happened, the teacher had smacked them. I couldn't help but be secretly pleased: these two are the nastiest boys in class.

Thursday, September 7
Fine weather

This morning we had Chinese. The teacher wrote a few questions on the blackboard and asked us to answer them. It's a matter of summarizing a text. He explained to us that if we don't know all the words, we can look them up in a dictionary.

I borrowed one from a friend because my father couldn't buy one for me. I was so busy consulting it that I forgot to write down the rest of the questions, which were then erased.

I asked my cousin, Ma Shiping, to lend me her notebook so that I could copy them out, but she refused. She thinks this is a test, and she doesn't want me to come in first.

It's a little thing, but it makes me realize that I can count on no one.

---

*Students must bring their own materials. The school has no supplies, few teaching aids, and no library.

Friday, September 8
A fair day

This morning during class, our Chinese teacher taught us that in life a man has to act according to two principles: his values and his dignity. This will ensure the respect of others.

At the end of class he warned us to be careful on the road on our way home. Those who have money can get a lift on a tractor for one yuan. The rest of us have to walk. But we mustn't dawdle.

Ma Yan and her parents in front of their ho

MA YAN'S FAMILY

Ma Yan's family is large. In addition to her paternal grandparents, the village of Zhangjiashu contains the families of her father's four brothers, whom Ma Yan designates according to their chronological age: "first uncle, second uncle," and so on.

Ma Shiping is her mother's cousin and is two years older than Ma Yan. Their stormy relationship is due to mutual admiration and jealousy. Despite her strong personality and good grades, Ma Shiping had to leave school at the end of the year and devote herself to domestic and farm work until she was married.

Ma Yan's father and mother are quite different from each other. Very tall, with a bowl haircut and taciturn, inhibited manner, Ma Dongji comes from a very poor family. Bai Juhua, Ma Yan's mother, comes from a more well-off family who lives twenty-two miles away. She is chatty and impulsive, with a ready smile and long hair hidden under the white scarf that identifies her as a Chinese Muslim.

Ma Dongji and Bai Juhua have three children; Ma Yan, thirteen in the year 2000, is the eldest. Her two brothers are Ma Yichao and Ma Yiting, ages eleven and nine in 2000.

Saturday, September 9
A fine day

This morning while we were watching a soap opera, my little brothers, who were playing outside, started to shout, "Our grandmother has arrived!"

My mother beamed. I went to join my brothers outside. We skipped rope and kicked a sandbag around. My grandmother and my mother stayed in the house alone. I don't know what they were talking about, but they laughed in a strange way.

Sunday, September 10
It's windy

This morning my grandmother and my parents went to the fair in Yuwang while I was still asleep. My little brothers turned everything upside down, and I was furious. But there's nothing to be done.

Monday, September 11
A fine day

This afternoon my cousin Ma Shiping came to fetch my brother Ma Yichao and me for the walk back to school.

Before letting us go, Mother stopped us to say, "You need to work hard. Even if I have to wear myself out, I'll pay for your studies, but on the condition that your grades are good."

My mother's words tug at my heart. I understand that everything she does is for us. I understand that we're her only hope. Nothing else counts but us.

I have to study hard to make a contribution to my country and my people one day. That's my goal. That's my hope.

Tuesday, September 12
Lovely weather

This afternoon I went out with a couple of classmates to run some errands. They're rich. They're always chomping away at one goodie or another. I watch them, but I can't afford to buy anything. Even chewing gum costs more than ten fen. That's far more than I can manage.

I suddenly realize why Mother hasn't gotten medical help before.* It's so that we can keep going to school. School costs tens of yuan all at once. Where does this money come from? It comes from the sweat and hard labor of my parents. Father and Mother are ready to sacrifice everything so that we can go to school. I must work really hard in order to go to a university later. Then I'll get a good job, and Mother and Father will at last have a happy life.

*Ma Yan's mother suffered from terrible stomach pains and sometimes spat blood. She was diagnosed with an ulcer and finally treated in 2002. At the time she wrote her diary, Ma Yan and her family did not know what was wrong with Bai Juhua.

Today after school my brother Ma Yichao and I went to find our mother. She was at the doctor's on Yuwang's main street. I wanted to leave straight after seeing her in order to get back to school and work. I just needed to stop and buy some shampoo. But Mother wouldn't let us go. She promised that when she was finished with the doctor, she would buy us something to eat.

All three of us went to the market. Mother bought us some food for dinner, but nothing for herself, so we had to eat it alone. I could clearly see that she was hungry and thirsty.

If she's depriving herself like this, it's so that we can live and work.

Thursday, September 14
Good weather

During math class this morning the teacher asked me to distribute the exercise books and to collect the workbooks. There were thirty-seven in all. None can be overlooked.

I don't want to be head of math.* But I can't refuse. I can't disappoint the teacher. I have to carry on doing everything I'm asked so that I can do well.

---

*There is a head student for each subject. The head collects and distributes homework and helps enforce discipline.

At eleven in the morning, after the last class of the day, we left school and went home for the weekend. The classes stop at the end of the morning to give us time to get back to our villages. There are seven of us, boys and girls. Two friends, Ma Yuehua and Ma Juan, take a tractor that costs one yuan. The rest of us, including my brother and my cousin, walk.

I'm always afraid on this road. The ravines on either side are very deep, the mountains dangerously steep. Sometimes thieves stop us and demand money.

Ma Yan's

THE ROAD HOME

Ma Yan's school is a twelve-and-a-half-mile walk from her village. In snow, rain, or blistering sun, Ma Yan and her brother Ma Yichao trudge along a dusty road that snakes through the hilly countryside. The route takes them past plowed fields, along a dangerous stretch bordered by a ravine, over steep climbs and descents, and then through a gap between yawning cliffs. It takes four hours if you walk quickly, five if you slow down.

The landscape offers little shelter in bad weather because few people live here. Often by the time the children arrive home, they are soaked through or frozen by glacial winds, their feet swollen. Even in snow or mud, Ma Yan wears canvas shoes that soak up water quickly.

The road can also hold unpleasant surprises. Once Ma Yan and her brother were held up by older teenagers who refused to let them pass unless they gave them bread, money, and their schoolbags. Ma Yan and her brother escaped by running off in different directions. Another time Ma Yan's youngest brother was hit and had to give up his school things, his pencils, and his eraser.

The children arrive home to a small brick house consisting of a single large room, of which half is taken up by the *kang*, the vast traditional bed, made of cement and heated from beneath. The whole family eats, sleeps, and lives on it.

There are few ornaments. Ma Yan and her brother's end-of-year diplomas hang on whitewashed walls. On top of a basic chest, two frames display family photos. The only luxury in the house is the black-and-white television set. An additional space serves as a kitchen and storeroom. In front of the house there's a small kitchen garden and a fenced area for animals: chickens, a donkey, and a few sheep.

This morning Mother went to the market in Yuwang. She was no sooner back in the house than she started shouting at my brothers and me. Then she began to get dinner ready: rice and salted cabbage. When we'd finished eating, she cried and cried.

I know why she's in tears. She's ill and she's the only one working in the fields right now. We're in the midst of harvest, and on top of that Mother has to look after the little ox she's bought to help till the land. Father is away, looking for work in Hohhot in Inner Mongolia.

If someone as brave as my mother cries when she's ill, how will the rest of us ever manage?

This afternoon my cousin, my brother, and I left to go back to school in Yuwang. When we arrived, the door of the dormitory wasn't open yet. We waited for quite a while before the porter turned up.

As soon as we were allowed in, Ma Shiping started to write in her diary.

"Will you be finished soon?' I asked her.

"No," she answered. "We can't all be as quick and clever as you."

She must have thought I was making fun of her.

I wonder why everyone is so displeased with me.

This afternoon my little brother Ma Yichao, who is in the same class as me, didn't line up properly for the gym class. The head of the class and the head of the gym rushed to give him a beating. The teacher permitted it.

Deep down, I'm in a rage. But what can I do? These two heads are the nastiest boys in the class.

If I study very hard and make daily progress, I'll go to a university and become a policewoman. And if these boys bend the law even a tiny little bit, I won't fail to have them punished.

This afternoon we had a music lesson. Ma Shengliang, Ma Xiaoping, and my brother Ma Yichao forgot their books.

The teacher told them off. "You're really stupid. You come here to work and you don't even bring your books!"

Then she tells the first two to leave the class and go and stand outside in the sun without moving. Only then does she begin our lesson.

Wednesday, September 20
A gray day

This afternoon the natural sciences teacher, Chen, gives us a lesson on nature. Ma Fulong talks and acts stupid at the back of the room.

The teacher pulls him up by the collar and tells him to sit up straight. Some of my friends say that the teacher is very nasty; others that he was right to discipline the student since one shouldn't talk in class.

I think the teacher is right, because on this road to our future life, we have to take the right track and not wander off on the wrong one.

Thursday, September 21
A fine day

This afternoon after school the class head orders us to go and get our meal in the kitchen. We had rice but no vegetables. I wanted to borrow some from my cousin, but she poured her entire ration of potatoes into her rice bowl and said there was no more.

"It doesn't matter," I said, and asked my friend, Ma Yuehua, for some vegetables. She grumbled a bit, but she's nicer than Ma Shiping and gave me a little.

I understand that you can't depend on relatives. If someone outside the family borrows something from you, then she'll remember you've done her a good turn. But if it's a member of the family, she won't want to lend you anything, even if you're unhappy. It's just not her problem.

At last I've cracked the nature of human relations. Everyone pays back their debts to others.

We came home from school this afternoon after the end of classes. After dinner Mother asked us to go to the buckwheat fields to bring back the bales that had already been cut. I couldn't really walk any farther, but Mother forced us to go. She had already harvested so much of the grain herself, how could we refuse her, especially since Father is still away working in Inner Mongolia.

It's in order to feed and clothe us that Mother works so hard. If it weren't for us, she wouldn't have to harvest buckwheat. It's right that she asks us and equally right that we help. Otherwise how would we be worth all the trouble she takes over us? She wears herself out so that we can have a different future from hers. She exhausts herself to provide food for us when there's nothing left, and then she exhausts herself all over again, without getting anything out of life for herself. She doesn't want us to live the way she does. That's why we have to study. We'll be happy. Unlike her.

RURAL POVERTY

Ma Yan's village is in one of the poorest parts of China, known as the Region of Thirst.

Persistent drought has led the government to declare the area uninhabitable. Despite the fact that daily life is a constant struggle for survival, about three million people still live here. The average annual income of the inhabitants of Ma Yan's village is around four hundred yuan (approximately forty-eight American dollars), a miserable sum compared to the Chinese average of six thousand yuan (approximately seven hundred twenty-five American dollars).

Since the land does not produce enough to support his family, Ma Yan's father tries to find work elsewhere. Like tens of millions of other peasants, he will hire himself out to work on construction sites in the cities or to labor for other farmers at harvesttime. He may be away from home for several months at a time to earn money.

Those whom Ma Yan calls "rich" are mostly children from the town of Yuwang rather than from the surrounding villages. Their parents are government workers or businesspeople, whose professions guarantee certain salaries and a social status above that of peasants. Ma Yan's "rich" have a real wardrobe, whereas she hasn't a single change of clothes; they have pocket money, whereas she can't even pay for vegetables to go with the rice she eats for lunch. Compared to people in the big cities, both groups are at the bottom of the social scale.

Peasants in the city are objects of ridicule. This is especially true in large cities like Shanghai or Beijing, but it is also true in small towns like Yuwang, where the inhabitants treat the peasants in the same way that they themselves are treated elsewhere.

Regional accents may betray the origin of a person, who becomes the object of contempt once his or her accent is singled out as not "noble" enough.

The village of Zhangjiashu

This morning I was in the middle of doing homework when Mother interrupted me.

"Come, we're going to husk the grain."

My big cousin Ma Yimei, my little cousin Ma Yifang, my two brothers, my mother, and I all work together on the stretch of land in front of our house.

Suddenly the son of Yang Dangqi arrives in a tractor with a full load of buckwheat, and he dumps his harvest in front of our house. Mother asks him to leave, but he just sneers. She asks a second time, and he still does nothing. She's very angry and she starts calling him names.

In my heart of hearts I think he's a scoundrel. He takes other people's places, pretending it's first come, first served. And it's useless for us to protest.

In these times even beggars need degrees. Nothing works for you if you don't study. In the big cities, even going to the toilet requires being able to read.

Sunday, September 24
A nice day

This afternoon on the way to school, we meet a man pulling an ox. He's accompanied by a second man who holds his jacket in his hand. They tell us about their childhood.

When they went to school, shepherds would stop them on their way and demand bread. They ask us if there are still people who block the road and don't let you pass. "Fewer than before," we say. "You're lucky," they say.

Monday, September 25
A gray day

At noon, in our history lesson, the teacher asks us several questions. I don't know any of the answers. Luckily he hasn't chosen me. He's singled out my brother and two other students, who don't know the answers either. Only Ma Shiping, tall and proud, with her long braid, answered correctly. The teacher complimented her. I admire her. She's so clever.

Tuesday, September 26
A gray day

A music lesson this afternoon. After the class the teacher organizes games for us. We play blindman's buff, and whoever is caught has to sing and dance. The first group creates a song-and-dance number, and then the second group does.

"Which of the two is better?" asks the music teacher.

Everyone agrees the second group was remarkable.

I have to take note of these girls and do well in all my classes, including music.

Wednesday, September 27
A fair day

This afternoon we went back to the dormitory after our classes. I saw that Ma Yuehua was writing something. The head of the dormitory, Ma Jing, asked her to clean the floor.

"I'll do it when I've finished my work," she answered, without lifting her nose from her book. The head of the dorm wouldn't take no for an answer. She insisted that Ma Yuehua clean up instantly. If she doesn't, she'll report her to the teacher.

Ma Yuehua weeps her rage.

Thursday, September 28
A gray day

This afternoon Ma Shiping, Li Qing, and I went to Yuwang to buy bread. In the first bakery we came to, the bread was very small, so we didn't buy any. We found a second bakery and decided to go in. I said, "I will have a piece of bread and a twisty doughnut."

The assistant handed them to me. When I was leaving the bakery, he made a joke behind my back.

Is it because we're country girls or because I pronounced the word *bread* badly? I'll never know.

At lunchtime when we leave for home, it's very cold. It's raining too. The other girls in my dorm are getting lifts home on a tractor. There's only my brother and me and one other pupil left walking.

We come to a spot where the water has washed away the strip of road and we can't get through. My brother puts his foot on a rock and leaps across, making it to another rock. He pulls me by the hand, and I get across too. In turn I give my hand to the other girl and pull her across to our side. We finally manage to get up the slope and are out of danger.

This morning, just after I had eaten a bowl of yellow rice for breakfast, I sat down to read *Voyage to the West*, which a school friend lent me. Suddenly I heard two tractors coming along the road toward our house.

People say that these two tractors will build up the road. This is really good news. Once this work is done, no one will any longer be able to say that we live "on the island of Taiwan."*

---

*The villagers joked that as the slope settled lower and lower, the family house, located on a small hill, was moving farther and farther away—just like the island of Taiwan was distancing itself (politically) more and more from mainland China.

Sunday, October 1
A fine day

This morning, on the day of the national holiday,* the weather is particularly beautiful. My maternal grandmother, who lives in a village to the north of Yuwang, is ill, and my mother decides to go and see her. But an hour later, she's changed her mind and no longer wants to go.

I ask her, "Why don't you want to go and see Grandmother?"

"I'll go tomorrow when I have to go to the market in Yuwang," she says.

I ask again, "Why, why don't you go today?"

"I'll go when I've done the housework."

"Don't worry about it," I say to reassure her. "I can do it. I'm big enough. Really."

Mother smiles. "You really are growing up!"

She finally did go to see Grandmother, on a bicycle she borrowed from her aunt, and with my youngest brother riding behind.

Monday, October 2
A fine day

This morning the men are repairing the road with their tractors. They don't know where to get earth to shore it up, and the road sinks lower and lower.

---

*October 1 marks the start of a week-long holiday celebrating the founding of the People's Republic of China.

A lot of people are watching from a safe distance and laughing. I don't know why they're laughing.

My cousin hears them and explains. "They're making fun. They're saying that when this road is finally finished, you'll definitely be living in Taiwan."

When she hears this, Mother is furious. She asks the workers to remove the earth from in front of our door in order to create a wide access road for us.

"Clear this earth away so that we can live!" she protests.

Once the earth has been used to shore up the track, some people start to mock again: "This is a really good road. What dreams Ma Dongji must have had." *

Really, people come up with the most ridiculous things these days!

Tuesday, October 3
A fine day

Very early this morning Mother wakes my brother Ma Yichao so that he can help her get the donkey ready for work. Mother walks in front, while my brother drives the donkey from behind. I can see all the wrinkles on my mother's face.

She's aging, and all because she wants to fill our stomachs and secure our future.

---

*The reference is to Ma Yan's father, who must have had a dream like the one in a Chinese legend in which a man dreamed that the mountain in front of his house was flattened.

Wednesday, October 4
A fine day

We're still home on vacation, and I'm in the process of doing my homework. Ma Shiping comes over to play. We play hide-and-seek with my brothers. I tell Ma Shiping that if she can find me, I'll explain one of the math problems to her. She replies that she knows all her math by heart and goes off.

I think to myself that, deep down, the only person I can count on is me.

Thursday, October 5
A fine day

This morning Mother wants to winnow the rice in order to remove the husks. When she opens up the rice bags, she finds mice in them. She flies off the handle and yells at us.

I was supposed to make sure the door to the storeroom was always closed and I forgot. The mice got in. And that's why Mother is so angry.

Friday, October 6
A fine day

This afternoon my mother, Ma Shiping, and my cousins were discussing things at home. After that, Ma Shiping, who is not much older than I am, asked me to turn on the tape recorder so that we could dance. I danced with one of my little cousins. At first no one else danced. But by the end everyone was twirling and their faces grew red with excitement. This was my happiest day.

Saturday, October 7
A gray day

This afternoon, after doing my other work, I started to do my homework. I heard my little brother Ma Yichao crying. He's stretched out on the bed. I ask him why he's crying. He says he didn't manage to do the exercises in his workbook. He still has to fill in the blank spaces. I help him do it.

After a little while, I tell him I need to do my own work now, and he must finish his on his own. If I don't finish it today, the teacher will reprimand me and hit me.

Mother walks by. "You're really very silly." She launches an attack on me.

I'm astonished. Why has she told me off like that? Have I said something really stupid? I feel terribly sad. Nothing is too much effort where her son is concerned, but I have to make do the best I can.

I feel so alone. There's no one to talk to.

Sunday, October 8
Rain

Today I came back to the dormitory with a few other students. I put down what I was carrying. Then I asked Ma Shiping to lend me her exercise book and explain a question to me. She pretended that she didn't understand it either.

I tried to look at her exercise book, but she pulled it away and swore at me.

Once again I have the feeling that everyone resents me, whereas I don't feel resentful of anybody. Perhaps I'm not seeing things very clearly.

I never lie. I'm not like Ma Shiping, who always tells lies, especially when she's done wrong. I shall have to work even harder so that I never have to ask anyone's help in understanding a question.

Monday, October 9
A gray day

This afternoon we had a Chinese test. The teacher said to us, "Work quickly and it will soon be over." My pulse raced. There was a question I didn't know how to answer.

I still haven't solved the problem.

Monday, October 23
Light rain

This morning after classes I went to the market in Yuwang with two friends. We saw a lot of people there who are very different from us. One doesn't have a leg; another is missing a foot. There's even a blind man.

I used to think I'd never survive in this school. And today I meet a blind man. A blind man manages to live, so why shouldn't I?

I have to get better and better and get ahead of everyone at school.

This afternoon our music teacher, the one with the long braid, gives us a lesson.

At the end she asks, "Who can tell us a story?" Everyone points to Yang Bin, a boy I like a lot. The teacher asks him to come up to the platform, but Yang Bin can't get to the end of his story. Hu Zhimin takes over, but he can't finish the story either. The teacher starts where he left off, but even she can't bring it to a conclusion. Finally she tells us another story called "The Fox Eats the Chicken." This is a funny story, and I'm drunk with laughter.

This afternoon our Chinese teacher asks us to sing, recite a poem, or tell a story.

I particularly liked the song my brother Ma Yichao sang, "Wait for the Day When You Say Good-bye."

We learned this song together when we were in the third year. The words give us courage. "At the moment when Mother and Father come to say good-bye, they declare, 'Child, I'm sending you on your way. Think no longer of your parents or of your beautiful native land.'"

I like this song very much because it was Mother herself who taught it to us. When I hear it, I always think of her.

Thursday, October 26

This afternoon, during the break after our first Chinese lesson, we skipped rope. Our Chinese teacher, Ma Shixiong, a man of about twenty-seven, who's very nice to us, stood and watched us. His face beamed with happiness, as if he were the same age as us. I haven't seen him this happy since the term started.

I think he's reminded of his childhood when he watches us. When he was a child, he probably played the same games, and played them well.

That's why, seeing us skipping, he remembers that happy time and looks so pleased.

Friday, October 27

We walk home in a light rain, which gradually eases.

I have a fight with Ma Shiping. She says I'm selfish, that I take other people's things, but when others borrow my school things, I call them copycats.

I reply, "Didn't you borrow my things? Didn't you take my exercise book? Who did you want to show it to?"

"I didn't take it. It was Xiao Hong," she answers.

I ask Xiao Hong, but she claims she's got nothing to do with it.

Ma Shiping is upset and says no more.

So I retort, "You even lie to yourself."

This morning the weather was beautiful. But after a while the snow started to fall. Blown by the wind, the flakes floated and danced in the sky.

Seeing the snow, I thought of one of my paternal grandmother's sayings: "If it snows at the beginning of October, the wheat harvest the following year will be good."

That's why I'm so happy to see snow. Let it snow a lot. The villagers will have water to drink and they won't need to go and fetch it from far away.

BITTER WATER

There is no running water in the village of Zhangjiashu. The villagers have two ways of stocking up. They gather rain and snow water, which they store in cement tanks dug into the ground, and there is also a well of "bitter water," located an hour's walk from the village. The water from this well is only good for watering the fields or for household tasks. It irritates the skin if you use it for washing.

Underground tanks hold drinkable water.

Several times a week the villagers walk to the well to fetch the bitter water in buckets that hang from a wooden stick balanced on the back of the neck. The buckets are heavy, and children like Ma Yan and her brother can manage to carry only a single bucket home.

According to Ma Yan's mother, it's best to arrive at the well before dawn if you don't want to wait in line for a long time. This means setting off at about four in the morning.

This morning it's very cold. I'm off to visit my paternal grand-mother, who lives with my fifth uncle in the village, and I stay for quite a while.

When I get home, Mother starts to reprimand me. "Why don't you prepare the vegetables you need for school yourself? You always wait for me to do it. Do you know where those little white rolls you like come from? Have you ever thought about it? I steam them for you and your brother, and then the rest of the family is deprived of wheat flour. You know very well we're going through hard times and that I'm ill. And on top of that you want me to wait on you. You're really heartless. I allow you to study, but you never think of me once you go to school."

All of these criticisms come out in any old order, and suddenly I'm angry. Other children pay a yuan to get a ride on a tractor to go to school. My brother and I always walk both ways.

But it's also true that we live in want. Without my mother, I would never have been able to go back to school. She doesn't look after her health and she makes it possible for us to study.

I really shall have to make my contribution to the country and have a good career so that my family isn't looked down on any longer.

Monday, October 30

This afternoon the last period of the day was a class assembly where all our group's problems were sorted out, whether they had to do with studying or health or dormitory life.

Ma Ping and Ma Shengliang had had a quarrel. The insults they hurled at each other were painful to listen to. Suddenly the teacher opened the door. A comrade by the name of Hu had told him what was going on. Now the teacher reprimanded both students. They squirmed on their bench, ill at ease, in danger of squashing it under their weight. None of which stopped the teacher from continuing his severe criticism.

I think he's right to do so. In order for there not to be any more quarrels or out-and-out fights, this is the best thing he can do to ensure the good behavior of the entire class.

Tuesday, October 31

This afternoon our music teacher taught us a new song, "The Sun." Then she asked us to sing everything we'd learned since our first lesson. When we had finished, she asked if anyone would like to sing alone. Everyone said that Ma Yichao sang very well.

I'm so pleased for him. I'm proud of having a talented brother, especially since I can't sing. Ma Yichao, who has a roguish manner, with his short hair and laughing eyes, is known throughout the school for his songs. Whenever anyone asks for a singer, the answer is invariably, "Ma Yan's brother."

My heart is full of joy, like a flower whose petals are opening.

It's a beautiful day. We're having our natural science class. The teacher reminds me of a teacher I had in my second year of elementary school. Their attitudes and gestures are very similar. When I see my current teacher, it makes me think of all the little attentions my old teacher paid me. So that I would have a good voice, he taught me to sing. So that I would be in good health, he had me do sports.

Chinese lesson this morning. The teacher hasn't prepared anything and he asks us to read the text ourselves. He picks Ma Chengmin, Ma Shilong, and Ma Shengliang. But these comrades don't quite manage to read the whole text. The teacher then chooses Li Xiaoyan. She reads beautifully.

The teacher calls on my brother twice, each time to answer a single question. He performs well and manages to give good answers. My anxiety is stilled. I was afraid my brother might make mistakes.

The teacher asks Bai Xue what *pretend* and *to never know* mean. Bai Xue answers. My pulse is racing. I'm worrying that I'll be next. I haven't even finished my thought when the teacher asks me to stand up. He asks, "Into how many parts can lesson twelve be divided?" I answer, "Into three parts: first, the preparation for writing the letter; second, writing the letter; third, the sending of the letter."

I fear that my answer may be wrong, but the teacher says, "Correct," and I relax a little. But the teacher continues to question me. "Is there anything else?" I give the right answer, and he says, "Correct, but you need to read the text some more."

This afternoon my brother and I went home.

It's very cold, and when we get there, no one's in. A neighbor tells us my mother went to see our paternal grandfather. My fifth uncle, a man who's as tall as my father and who has had seven daughters, is building a house. My brother and I put on padded jackets that keep us very warm and go off to our grandfather's.

A lot of people are gathered to help build the house. The wind is so strong, it's hard to keep our eyes open. We go into the house. Mother is busy cooking. She gives us two bowls of vegetables and tells us to eat up.

A little later my grandfather comes in too. Mother gives him a bowl as well. Grandpa sits down on a stool and starts to eat. His eyes are full of tears from the wind. His cotton jacket and his shirt are so dirty, it's best not to look at them. When I look at my grandmother, I think that she's even more pitiful than he is. Her hair is all white; a towel full of holes covers her head. On top of this, she's carrying two of my fifth uncle's daughters in her arms. The children kick against her hard.

How can Grandmother bear it? How her arms must ache. . . . In her place, I'd be in agony.

If I manage to get through my studies and find work, I'll

certainly take my grandparents into my house so that they can lead a happier life. Then they won't have to put up with fifth uncle's constant bad temper. I just fear they won't be able to hold on that long. But that would mean that they're condemned to a miserable old age, without ever having had the chance to lead a good life.

Ma Yan with her paternal grandpa

MA YAN'S GRANDPARENTS

When Ma Yan wrote these entries, her paternal grandfather, Ma Shunji, was eighty. His father had been a beggar who went from village to village begging alms. As a small child, Ma Shunji accompanied him. But when he turned four, his father sold him for forty-four pounds of rice and a handful of seeds to a rich landowner from Zhangjiashu who had no children of his own at the time. Ma Yan's grandfather worked on the landowner's farm from the age of seven until, at the age of twenty, he was given up to the army by his adoptive parents in 1941. He fought in the Chinese Revolution and in the Korean War, returning to Zhangjiashu in 1953.

On the eve of his departure from his village, Ma Shunji had been married to a thirteen-year-old girl who, like him, was an orphan sold off to a large family. She waited for his return from the army for twelve years. Almost fifty years later, they are still living together in Zhangjiashu, after having had five boys, one of whom is Ma Yan's father.

Ma Yan's mother's family is much "richer" than that of her father.

"We had more to eat in the family house," Bai Juhua says. "When I saw my husband's father's house, small and dark and neglected, I wondered how an army veteran could live so badly. I was surprised that his life was so hard."

She also remembers the hostility of the villagers, who had only contempt for her in-laws. " 'Useless people,' they said to me. I was advised to divorce and leave." She stayed and became the pillar of her family.

Ma Yan's maternal grandparents criticize the paternal branch a great deal and rarely come to visit their daughter at home. The rivalry between the two families is one of Ma Yan's motives for studying. She wants her mother's family to stop being contemptuous of her father and to prove that his children can succeed.

This morning Father came back from far away.* I suggested that I make a meal for him, but he said no. He had to go and help fifth uncle build his house. He immediately went out again. There's only my brother and me in the house. I put a low table on the *kang* and do my homework there.

My little brother is playing outside. A little while later other children come and play with him and then go away. When I've finished my work, I go and look for my brother. Hu Xiaoping, the son of a neighbor, tells me that he went off to fifth uncle's house. I sit around for a bit, but then I get so bored that I go there too. Father and a lot of the other villagers work until nightfall. Then the others clamber down the house frame, eat, and go back home.

Only my father and my little brother are still at work. They carry on until nine o'clock. Why don't they stop? I ask.

My fifth aunt, Uncle's wife, answers me. "Your father only arrived at noon so he hasn't done much work. And here you are telling him to stop already."

I should have replied, "Last year when we built our house, you only came to help in the afternoons. Did we say anything? You don't even know how to tell good from bad. You and us, we're not the same. We're not the same at all."

But I didn't say a word.

*Ma Yan's father had been away working on a construction site in Inner Mongolia for the last three months.

This afternoon we were still at home, even though we should have been on our way to school. But our little bread rolls weren't ready. My brother and I decided to leave in any case and locked the door. We went to find Father in the village, to give him the key, and he advised us to wait until we'd eaten before leaving. I told him Ma Shiping said we had to leave early today because we might be able to hitch a ride on a tractor.

My brother says he's hungry and thirsty. He sits down and waits for something to eat. My father gives me ten yuan to buy some bread with. I run into a shop to get change for the money and give five yuan back to my father. The rest will be enough for bread.

I suddenly think that it has taken my father such hard work to earn these yuan. He's given his sweat and blood for them, working in Inner Mongolia. How can I take them just on a whim? I must work harder and make it to a university, and get a good job. Then I'll never again be weighed down and saddened by these questions of money.

This afternoon, I'm busy reading my Chinese manual when the bell rings to announce the end of the period. All my friends go out to play. A little while later, several of them come back to say that there's going to be a Chinese test. My heart starts racing. People are getting their books out to look through them because the questions in the test will certainly be in there somewhere.

And then someone claims the test will be on a wholly different subject and on a separate sheet of paper.

I don't trust myself, so I carry on studying the book.

The lesson starts. The teacher comes in empty-handed. He says we're going to have a class assembly instead of a test. I'm so happy. Full of joy like a bud blossoming into flower. I'm no longer afraid.

Tuesday, November 7

Music lesson this afternoon. The teacher gives us a new song to learn, "Little Tadpole." It's a lovely song. "Little tadpole, big head, tiny body, small tail, lives in the water and grows until he's utterly transformed."

The teacher sings it a few times with us, then asks us to sing it without her. We sing in chorus for a few minutes, then the teacher asks us to sing one by one. "Who's a good singer?" she asks, and the pupils all shout out in unison, "Li Xiaoyan, Bai Xue, Ma Zhonghong, and Ma Xiaojun."

The teacher with the long braid asks my brother Ma Yichao, "Why don't you sing for your comrades? What do you all think?" Everyone approves.

My brother gets up and sings. He's very funny, and everyone bursts into laughter. He isn't the person he used to be. He's become a comedian. He tells funny stories. He likes playing the clown.

In this school we only learn one song a week. "Little Tadpole" is the one I like singing most of all.

It's beautiful this morning. My father came from the village and brought bread for my brother and for me. After class I went to the market with my brother. My father's already there waiting for us. I ask him why he asked us to meet him here. He says he wants us to have one very good meal.

He takes us to one of the little restaurants on Yuwang's main street, orders two bowls of rice cooked in a meat soup, and tells us to eat. Afterward he also buys us some apples, telling us we're to eat them with our evening bread.

On the road back to school, I meet my great-uncle and his wife, my second uncle and his wife, my third uncle, and my maternal grandfather. They say to me, "So you went to market too." I say yes.

They don't invite my brother and me to eat with them. I think about this. How good it is to have parents! Without parents, you're an orphan and there's no one to take care of you and love you.

How wonderful it is to have parents and their love!

This afternoon it's beautiful out. Our last class is natural sciences. Everyone rushes in when it begins. But my cousin Ma Shiping and I drag our feet for a bit in the courtyard. I see the teacher arriving and I rush like crazy and get into the classroom just behind him.

The moment I come in, the other children get up to greet the teacher. I rush to my place so as not to miss anything. After the class the teacher distributes our notebooks and assigns the homework for the next lesson. He adds, "When you've finished, don't leave the room. Your Chinese teacher still has a few things to say to you."

I fear that we may be having a surprise test. But, in fact, it's only so that we can do an exercise in our workbooks. He warns us that tomorrow morning inspectors will be coming around to examine our work.

Friday, November 10

This afternoon we made the trek home after school. My mother was preparing noodles for my brother and me. My father was outside, busy mixing water with coal dust. With the mud it makes, we create coal cakes to burn.

My brother and I went off to visit our paternal grandmother, who lives at our fifth uncle's. My grandparents live in the big room. My uncle has dug a sort of cave next to the house for his seven children.

When we arrive, our grandmother is out. Our cousin tells us that our grandparents are busy cutting fodder for the ox. We go off to help them. When he's finished cutting the grass, Grandfather feeds it to the ox. Grandmother invites us into the kitchen and offers us bread and steamed potatoes. I accept half a roll, and my brother has a potato.

My grandmother's almost eighty but she still works for fifth uncle's family. So does my grandfather. Old people who have an education certainly don't have to do this kind of work. Surely when one reaches old age, it's time to benefit from life. Nowhere but here do you see old people serving the young like this.

It's obvious that one has to study these days in order to avoid the fate of my grandparents, who have to slave away into their old age. They'll never taste happiness.

It's very cold this afternoon. My father comes back from the market. He puts his bags on the ground and climbs up onto the *kang*. Sitting on the bed, he grumbles, "It really is very cold today! So cold you can't take your hands out of your pockets."

I ask him what's in the bags. My little brother Ma Yiting jumps off the bed to go and look. He sees a padded jacket, a pullover, and some colored tiles for the house. He asks who the jacket and the pullover belong to, and my father says, "They're for your sister and your big brother."

My youngest brother then starts to cry. My father promises him that on the next market day, he'll buy one for him. Reassured, he stops crying. Then my mother speaks to him harshly for asking for things from his father, and Ma Yiting starts crying again.

My mother must be suffering from her stomach pains today. Otherwise, why chide the little one like that?

This afternoon Ma Shiping, Ma Yichao, and I were all on our way to school together when we were stopped at the intersection of Hujiashu village by five or six big boys who asked us where we were going.

My brother answered that we were going to school in Yuwang.

"What year are you in?" they asked.

"Why do you want to know?" my brother retorted.

These boys were not from our village and suddenly they got mean. The youngest of them threw stones at us. The biggest hurled insults. We started to run as fast as we could until we got to the ravine. There we saw some shepherds tending their flocks. Once again, I grew very frightened. But when I looked at the shepherds more closely, I could see they were adults. I calmed down.

My palms were damp, as if I'd just come out of the water.

Monday, November 13

It's a beautiful afternoon, and our final period is devoted to a class assembly. The teacher asks the student responsible for our communal life to organize us so that the school is kept thoroughly clean. The head boy tells the boys to sweep the yard, and the girls to clean the windows. Ma Jing, Ma Donghong, and Li Qing sweep the yard. I let them do it and then clean up the dust.

Every time I pick up a broom and a dustpan, I think of my family. We clean the floor in the same way. I remember the first time my mother taught me to sweep. She explained, "When you sweep the ground, it's best to sprinkle it with a bit of water first, then you wait a moment before beginning." Mother held my two hands. She advised me to bend a little at the waist. That way I wouldn't make the dust fly.

I remember each of her words as if they were spoken yesterday.

Another beautiful afternoon. Our last lesson is music. The teacher comes in, and the head boy barks, "Get up. Good afternoon, teacher."

The teacher replies, "Good afternoon, comrades. Sit down. Today, we're going to learn 'At the Sound of the Little Drum.'"

The teacher repeats the song several times, then asks us to sing. We sing badly, so she repeats it again. Then she says, "You'll sing it again after class. That way you'll know it well."

She also says, "I heard that you would soon have your midterm exam. Is that right?"

All the comrades answer, "Yes."

The music teacher allows us to study our work so that we will get good results the next day. When I hear her give us permission to do this, it's as if I'd received a dose of mother love.

Wednesday, November 15

It's snowing hard this afternoon. In our first period, the math teacher comes in and announces, "Today we'll be taking the midterm exam." My heart starts hammering.

We have to solve problems and fill in the blanks. For the most part, it seems quite easy to me.

The teacher announces, "I read; you write." As we go on, the problems get harder and harder. I'm no longer able to fill in some of the blanks. I can't even do a simple calculation. I do the best I can.

After class I compare my answers to those of others. But none of my answers match theirs.

Mother, all the hope you've put in me has been in vain. I'll try and give you more satisfaction later on, okay, Mother? I promise. I'll try and get better results in the future.

Thursday, November 16

Our first two classes are in Chinese grammar and spelling. The teacher explains, "You'll review during the next two lessons and then next week you'll take your Chinese exam."

This makes me think of yesterday's exam. When the teacher distributed the papers, at first glance everything looked simple. So I started to answer the questions. But toward the end I ran into more and more problems.

No sooner had the Chinese teacher uttered the word *exam* than I no longer had the heart to carry on reading my book. Do you want to know why? Yesterday I went to the office of the math teacher. His niece and his two twin daughters were just looking over my paper, corrected by the teacher. I got eight answers wrong. There were not that many questions to start with, and I got eight of them wrong! I can hardly be lighthearted after that.

I also saw Bai Xue's paper. I had the feeling that I was the lowest of the low, and she had walked in the heavens. What a distance there was between us. It was as if I had never existed.

When night falls Mother heats up some water and tells me to wash my hair. My paternal grandmother is ill, she explains. She's got pains in her kidneys and her legs. My two brothers have gone off to see her.

When the water is finally hot, I wash my hair. Ma Yichao comes home alone, his hands covering his face.

Mother asks him, "Did you really go to Grandmother's? You saw her?"

"No," he replies.

"Why ever not?"

He explains. "Grandfather had been to the mosque at Liwazi, more than a mile from the village. They'd given him a present of meat pancakes. When Ma Yiting and I reached his door, he shouted at us. 'It's so cold outside. Why on earth have you come?'"

There was little point in repeating that they'd come to see their grandmother. He sent them away because, he said, it was so cold. So my brothers came home.

Mother starts to criticize Grandfather. "How can we look after him if he behaves like that?"

But I think she's wrong. Grandfather will never change. He doesn't understand that we want the best for him. When my mother criticizes him, I feel terrible. Why do none of his daughters-in-law understand what's going on inside him? He's always been like this. I hope I'll never hear another bad thing said about my grandfather.

It's very cold this afternoon. The snow is falling thickly, and there's a gusting wind. Father came back from the market, where he bought two bags of wheat. He's also got other things, which he's carried in a big sack. He comes into the room and puts down his bundle. Mother takes out the vegetables, garlic, noodles. She looks right down into the bottom of the bag, where she finds one or two pounds of meat. She asks Father why he thought it was a good idea to buy meat. He explains, "Today the children are all home together. Let's have a feast. They don't eat well at school. That's why I bought a little meat for them."

So Mother makes a soup with rice and meat for us. While we're eating, she comes out with one of her sayings. "Liver isn't meat. A nephew isn't a descendant. The son must give birth to himself. The tree must have deep roots."

Ma Yan and her family on the *kang*, their large cement bed

No matter how much I think about the meaning of these phrases, I understand nothing at all.*

This afternoon, just before we have to leave for school, my brother Ma Yichao recounts what happened to us last Sunday on our way to school; how we were attacked by five youths from another village. After she's listened to us, Mother asks Father, who hasn't gone off to his work outside the village yet, to accompany us. Father hoists our provisions on his shoulder. We each take our schoolbag, but I'm also carrying my brother's clothes and shoes.

We set off on our long trudge of several hours through the snow. When we get to the top of the plateau, Father's ears are already very red. We're walking in silence. I hear his tread and I see the snow on his leather shoes.

I think of my exam results. How can I possibly merit the long walk Father is making for our sakes? He's afraid we'll be beaten up on the way. I'm going to study harder now, be successful, then go off to university and find work. I must pay Father back for this walk and give him and Mother the gift of a better life.

*Bai Juhua's saying means that one's own children are the most important thing to a man or woman.

This morning our first lesson is a study period where we can do our homework and read over our texts. The Chinese teacher warns us, "Study your lessons well. Our next period will be the Chinese exam."

All the comrades launch themselves into studying. When the time for the next period arrives, the teacher comes into the classroom and distributes the test papers. I can see that it's easy and I settle right in. While I'm writing, I tell myself that I absolutely must do well for Mother and Father's sake and get a top grade.

The time comes to hand in our papers. I ask the others how many checkmarks they had—that is affirmative answers—and how many Xs—the negative answers. They say three Xs and one checkmark. Does that mean I've once again made mistakes? Mother and Father's hope vanishes into the distance once more.

I shall have to study more.

The last lesson this afternoon is music. The teacher writes out the lyrics to songs on the blackboard. The first is called "I Have a Sheep." While the teacher writes, she leans her head against the blackboard, as if she's ill. It's clear that she has a headache. Writing is a strain, and she barely gets through all the stanzas.

The second song is "Wooden Rattles." The teacher gives the song sheet to Hu Zhimin and asks him to write it out for her. She sits down. I don't know what's wrong with her, but she seems very unwell. She looks as if she could pass out at any moment.

Hu Zhimin has copied out the words on the board, and the teacher gives us the tune. Then she asks us to sing on our own. We don't quite get to the end. She makes us repeat it all several times, then confides, "Ma Huiping, in class three of the fifth year, sings really well."

The meaning of this, from what I can gather, is that we should try and follow her example.

The teacher has worn herself out, and we still can't sing the whole song. It's not fair to her. Despite her illness, she's come to teach us so that we can take our turn in tomorrow's celebrations.

THE YOUNG PIONEERS' LETTER

The following letter is part of Ma Yan's activity with the Young
Pioneers, a national and international youth organization. In
the letter, she makes references to Mao Zedong (1893–1976),
founder of the People's Republic of China, and Jin Zhanlin, a
local hero who died several years ago.

Ma Yan in class, looking through the window

THE LETTER

On the afternoon of November 21 all the Pioneers at the school celebrated the anniversary of President Mao Zedong's telling us to follow the example of Grandfather Jin Zhanlin. In order to celebrate the spirit of Jin Zhanlin, who helped others; in order to learn what his good works meant; and so that we contribute our own love, we must:

1. Give books to other young comrades so that they too learn from the example of Grandfather Jin Zhanlin and do good.
2. Learn to do housework and help our parents.
3. Conscientiously protect public property.

All the Young Pioneers in the school need to follow the example of Jin Zhanlin and offer up their love. If we live, it's in order to improve the lives of others.

All the Young Pioneers of the school
November 21

The last class of the day is given up to the activities of the Young Pioneers. Hu Zhimin is the organizer. He picks out names at random. He asks Ma Shiping to get up and sing. At first she refuses. I'm pleased, because she made fun of me and said I sing like a little pig. Today, when the teacher asks her, she sings, but she's worse than I am.

When my turn comes, the teacher asks me to sing "The Dream Butterfly":

> *"Beautiful butterfly of my dream,*
> *fly among the others,*
> *fly through the pretty flowers. . . ."*

All the comrades say I've sung well, and that I could become a star. . . .

Secretly I'm very pleased. As of today I've got more confidence in my ability to sing. I shall have to carry on and do even better. I don't want to hear anyone imply that I sing like a pig.

I'm busy correcting a text this afternoon when the school day comes to an end. Ma Yichao brings food and calls me to come and eat.

A lot of comrades confide their admiration to me: "How kind your brother is! He brings you food and lets you eat first. He eats your leftovers. After your meal he goes to get water so that you can wash your bowl. . . ."

I'm so pleased by their words.

But today my brother has only brought rice without any vegetables. Halfway through the meal, Ma Shiping gives me a spoonful of her vegetables. I take a mouthful and give the rest to my brother.

At that moment I suddenly understand the true meaning of a sense of family. What the love of a mother is.

Friday, November 24

Before lunch my father and mother came to school to see my brother and me. They brought us a little rice and asked us to give it to our main teacher, that is, our Chinese teacher.

The bell announcing class rings. When lessons are over, my brother and I race down the road, but my parents are already leaving to see our maternal grandmother. They've heard she's still ill, which is why they want to go and see her. They give me a yuan to buy some apples to have with our evening bread.

Today I'm very sad. Do you want to know why? Because this morning my parents told me that when I got home, I had to feed the ox. I refused. But when I got home, I did feed the ox. The work has left my hands all rough and swollen. They're horrible to look at. And so I'm led to reflect: I've fed the ox once, and my hands are already rough. Mother feeds him every day—which explains why her hands are so swollen. Everything she does is for my brothers' and my future.

I want to cry and can't say a word. Please come back, Mother and Father. I need your love! I was wrong, okay? Come back quick. I'm thinking of you. Please come back.

My parents said they would be back from my maternal grandparents' today. My brothers and I got up very early. We prepared the food for the ox. Then I cooked for all of us. After we'd eaten, we stayed on the *kang* to watch TV. After that we went out to play.

Soon the sun set behind the mountain. But Father and Mother still didn't appear. We made some supper for ourselves and ate. After that my brothers stayed at home to watch cartoons, but I was worried so I went out, without quite knowing where I was going.

Seeing me in this state, my brother went to find our second uncle's daughter, so that she could keep us company. We chatted for a bit, then my brothers and I went to bed without saying another word.

A house without grown-ups doesn't feel normal. Children are always children. My father and mother have gone, and I feel desperate. I hope they come back soon.

Sunday, November 26

This afternoon when we got to school, the dormitory was still locked. Only Ma Juan is there, a friend from our class. We sit down in front of the dormitory. After a while, another comrade arrives, Ma Yuehua. She asks us why we don't go in. We tell her the door is still locked. She has the key, she tells us. We go in and put down our bags. We open our books and start to read.

A little while later a motorbike, driven by a man, pulls up outside. Yang Xiaohua has been given a lift all the way to school. Both of them come to the dormitory.

The man asks, "Is your stove working?"

"No," we answer.

He asks us why we don't light the coal stove.

"The hearth is too full," we explain.

He takes off his jacket and starts to clean out all of last week's ashes. I ask myself who this man could be and why he's busying himself with getting our stove going. It turns out he's Yang Xiaohua's father. He's a nice man. When he dies, he'll certainly go to heaven.

Of course, this is only in my imagination. . . .

Monday, November 27

This afternoon the last period is given up to a class meeting. The teacher asks us to clean the school. Some comrades concentrate on the yard, others simply play. I study in the classroom. The student responsible for communal life comes in to tell me to go out. I go. During my absence, the floor is swept. I return to the classroom and carry on with my homework. He calls me again, this time to tell me to clean the windows. I go out and start wiping them. After that I return to the classroom once more.

He calls me yet again to tell me to go and do some dusting elsewhere. When I don't answer, he comes up close and smacks me. I still don't say anything. He hits me harder and harder. I pick up my little ruler and hit him across the face. Then I go off to do the dusting. I'm furious. If I become a good policewoman tomorrow and this boy commits a crime, I'll arrest him and shoot him. I'll cut him up with a knife!

Tuesday, November 28

Mother and Father, forgive me. Why do I ask for your forgiveness straight away? Because this afternoon our Chinese teacher, the most important one, lectured us: "Last week you took your midterm exams. Several comrades performed very well, but the vast majority of you had very poor results. You, the boarders, every week you bring a bag of rolls with you and once a term, a sack of rice. Do you think you deserve as much? Not even bread and rice. As for the rest of you . . ."

When the teacher gives out the test results, I can't lift my head. I haven't even come in second. Will I ever be able to hold my head up high again?

But I have to be confident. In the final exams I'll certainly have better results to show my parents.

Wednesday, November 29

This morning the math teacher came in with thirty-seven work-books in his hand. The atmosphere is bizarre. It really is. The teacher takes a handful of these exercise books and starts in: "I've already told you that if you haven't done the necessary work, there's no point handing it in!"

The top notebook belongs to Li Qing. The teacher asks her to get up and leave the class. She refuses. The teacher slaps her with the back of his hand across the neck. Then he slaps each of us one after another. He has one last exercise book in his hand. It belongs to Ma Fulu. The teacher orders him forward and, without saying a word, hits him.

I'm secretly very happy about this, because Ma Fulu has hit other comrades. And today it's the teacher's turn to slap him. He knows now what it feels like, knows just how pleasant it is! Might he now give up the habit of roughing us up? I so hope he'll never hit us again.

Thursday, November 30

Chinese class this morning. As soon as the teacher comes in, he asks if anyone present has any glass marbles. These are not allowed in school. The class head indicates one comrade, then another and another. The teacher confiscates a whole handful of marbles before at last beginning the lesson.

Lesson 22, "The Golden Bait: A War Narrative." The teacher announces that he's going to read the text and that we'll then analyze its meaning. While the teacher reads, I can't hold back my tears. Because my grandfather is just like one of the veterans in the story who've come back from the war in Korea. He, too, crossed the steppes, climbed mountains of snow. In fact, he resembles the old squadron chief quoted by our teacher—a man who persevered until the ultimate victory.

I'm proud of him, and my tears flow in homage to his bravery.

This afternoon after school it was very cold. My brother and I got our bags and went to the market. When we arrived, there were no tractors going to our village. We looked around a little longer, and I finally spied one. We got up into the trailer at the back. I thought to myself that it was easy enough getting in, but it would be harder getting out, because we would have to pay.

My parents didn't come to town today. Neither my brother nor I have any money. That's why it'll be difficult.

I've barely finished thinking this, when Mother approaches without our knowing. She murmurs, "You're dying of cold, aren't you?"

I turn around and see her. I'm thrilled. As soon as Mother gets on, the tractor takes off.

On the road the wind is very strong. My cheeks are bright red. Mother puts her hands on them. Right away, I feel warmer.

Mother is being so attentive. When I think of my exam results, I don't know how I'm going to tell her.

At dusk, when the fast is over, we're all watching a cartoon on the television: *Sun Child*. I go out to see what Mother is up to. I pull back the curtain on the door and see that she's making little potato dumplings for our dinner. I return to watch more of the cartoon with my brothers.

A little while later I want to go and help Mother. But she's already finished preparing the vegetables and rolls. There's only the rice left to cook.

"Can I help, Mother?" I ask.

"It's not worth it. Better go and do your homework."

I go back to do some writing.

While I write, I think. What a lot of trouble our parents go to for us. And couldn't we go to just a little trouble for them? So that they can have happy times in which they'll be the ones looked after by others.

RELIGIOUS PRACTICES

Ma Yan lives in a region of China defined by the Islamic faith of the Hui people, distant descendants of the Arab or Persian merchants and diplomats who came to China from the seventh century on. Today the Hui are similar to the ethnic majority of Chinese, the Han, with whom they share a language. Only their religious practice and certain of its outward signs, like the wearing of distinctive white head coverings, distinguish them from the majority of Chinese.

The village of Zhangjiashu is 100 percent Hui. There the imam, the local Islamic religious leader, is certainly one of the figures of authority, along with the traditional representatives of the government.

Although many of Ma Yan's schoolmates are also Hui Muslims, she is one of the few who observe the fast for the Muslim holiday of Ramadan. Ma Yan's family, while not particularly religious, respects tradition. Her mother wears the white head scarf of the Huis, as do almost all the women of the village. She also forbids her daughter to wear skirts or to show her bare arms.

At their house, there are no religious symbols—no pictures of Mecca, no holy verses from the Koran on the walls—which is the practice in more pious households. Fasting for Ramadan and respecting the other holidays associated with it are the only suggestions of religious observance in Ma Yan's journal.

Ma Yan's classmates jog past the Yuwang mosque, the local Muslim house of wors

This afternoon I washed my hair and got ready to go. Mother asked us to stay till the end of the afternoon. At the big mosque in Liwazi, more than a mile away, and in the little one, just behind us, prayers are going on to mark the end of the fast. If we wait, we can get something to eat before heading off.

We stay and sit on the bed. Suddenly I hear someone calling me. It's Ma Shiping, who's asking whether we're ready to go. I suggest she come in and wait with us, so that we can eat.

Mother has our cases ready, and after having served out the food, orders us straight off. It's already dark.

The moment we leave, I feel very sad. Tears stream down my face. I'm desolate about leaving home.

On the black, nighttime road, I fall behind. A little farther on, the other two decide on an alternative route, saying that on the first one we might get stopped. I follow them. After we've walked a little more, Ma Yichao suggests that next time we should get a tractor for one yuan. I agree. Ma Shiping doesn't. She wants to carry on walking to school.

We trail behind her. It's so dark that after a little while we lose sight of her. We run to catch up with her, but we still can't see her. I start to cry loudly. When we finally find her, I'm so happy, I burst into laughter.

Ma Shiping refuses to be intimidated by potential danger. She won't give in to it. Even if her life is at stake, she carries on. I admire her with all my heart.

Today after school the others went home. Ma Jing and I did our homework quickly, then went to the market. In a little shop I bought a notebook for my Chinese class and a smaller one for my diary. Ma Jing bought a few hairpins and a towel.

By chance I meet a relative, holding a big bag in her hand. She tells me my mother asked her to bring us some padded clothes that would keep us really warm. I open the bag and see that Mother has also sent along some doughnuts cooked in the fat from yesterday's feast.

I'm thrilled. Tonight I'll be able to eat lots. But I ask myself whether we'll be able to return my mother's kindness when she gets old.

Let's hope so. . . .

Music lesson this afternoon. The teacher warns us, "Study well, because next week we're having a test." Everyone starts to study. My heart sinks. As soon as the word *test* is mentioned, I feel like crying.

Why cry? Because I didn't come in at the top of the class in math or Chinese in the midterm exams. When I told my parents about this, Father didn't say anything. He simply walked out of the house. But Mother exploded. "If you carry on doing badly, you won't even deserve the rolls you take along each week."

Even though Father didn't say anything, I think he's angrier than Mother. That's why I have to do well in the music test next week. I have to bring at least one good grade home to my parents.

Wednesday, December 6

This morning it's beautiful out. Beginning the day's fast for Ramadan, the girls in the dorm tell each other funny stories. We've lit the incense we all bought together and we watch it burn. We tell each other we can soon go home and ask our mothers to make us noodles and rolls, so that we don't go around starving all the time.

When I hear a comrade say this, I feel really bad. It reminds me that I didn't come in first in the class. How will I be able to face going home and eating the meals Mother prepares?

But I have confidence in myself. At the end-of-term exams, if I don't come in first, I must at least come in second.

Thursday, December 7

The last class of the day is natural sciences. Then the comrades go out to play. I stay back to do my homework. Suddenly Ma Xiaohong and Ma Shiping, who are in my class, come in and ask, "What are you up to?"

Ma Xiaohong doesn't move, but Ma Shiping tears the notebook out from under me while I'm still writing. The word scrawls off, the notebook is torn, the pencil broken.

I'm so angry I can't keep it back. I swear at her, insult her. She pays me back in kind. I get so furious I can't even speak any longer. She goes away.

Ma Jing says, "Your cousin is really angry."

I answer, "Too bad. It's her fault in any case!"

But in my heart, it's as if I'm the guilty one, because she's older than me and I owe her some respect. My explosion was over the top. That's probably why I feel I'm in the wrong.

Friday, December 8

This afternoon after school Ma Shiping, my brother, and I get ready to put our things away and go off to the market. We see several tractors from our village. We decide to have a look around first, but when we come back, there isn't a single tractor left. We run through all the streets. My brother is really angry. He starts swearing. We keep looking for a vehicle, but then my brother disappears, so we have to look for him. We finally find him and also a tractor going near our village. All three of us get up onto the little trailer behind.

The driver's father asks us to divide ourselves up onto three tractors. "You can't all stay here with us. Where will the gas come from? We're the ones who pay for it."

These words make me see red. I'd like to jump off and look for another ride, but there is no other tractor around. I have to stay put and listen to the man.

The tractor heads off, and the noise of the engine drowns his voice. I can't hear him anymore. I lower my head and end up falling asleep. When I wake up, we're almost home.

When we get off, I take a yuan out of my bag and give it to the driver's father. He looks at us with contempt.

I think to myself, *Don't take all of us for poor penniless people. Some pupils are rich, some poor. And don't take me for a nobody. If I have to answer back and stand up for myself, I will. Don't mistake all students for people who don't know how to respond to insults, or how to fight. I'm not like the others. If someone offends me, I'll remember his name forever. I'll never forget.*

Saturday, December 9

Tonight we got up before daybreak to eat and start our fast for the day. My father said his prayers. I helped Mother with the cooking.

I put the big pot on the stove. Mother takes a little flour, mixes it with water. She wants to make sweet noodles.

She asks Father what he wants to eat. He says he'll have the same as we do. Mother takes a smidgen of water and starts to knead the pastry. When she mixes the flour, her hand starts to give her trouble, and she asks me to take over. She's in so much pain.

I come over to help her, but then she stops me. "No, it's not worth it. Go and finish your schoolwork first or you'll end up doing badly tomorrow."

So I go and do my homework. But in fact, I can't work. I watch Mother. Her hand hurts. But she has to cook now to prepare for the fast. She's such a kind and courageous woman. She treats her major illness like a minor one, even though she suffers

83

from hideous stomach pains. She takes pleasure in helping others. To me, she's nobility itself.

Sunday, December 10

This afternoon Mother made a little food, a few vegetables, so that we could leave for Yuwang before sunset. If we don't make it back to school tonight, it will be serious. We won't be present for the first class tomorrow, and the teacher will hit us. I ask Mother to heat up the vegetables quickly and to put the rolls in a bag.

But everything is already prepared. I haven't quite finished washing my hair, and she finds time to help me.

Father and Mother decide to accompany us part of the way. When the moment comes to leave them, my throat tightens. Me, I'm working for my own future, but why are my parents taking so much trouble for us? Do they hope that their children's lives will be better than their own? Or is it simply that they want us to honor them? Sometimes I really can't understand them.

Monday, December 11

After school today my brother and I finish off our homework. I ask my cousin if she'd like to come to the market with us.

"Yes, very much," she says.

All three of us leave. In the street I meet my fifth uncle and ask him whether my father has come to town. Yes, he says. He's just bumped into him.

While my brother and I look for our father everywhere, we manage to lose Ma Shiping.

Fifth uncle has told us that Father came to buy vegetables to mark the end of the fast of Ramadan, and we search high and low. Finally we find him. He still hasn't bought anything. I ask him why. He says he's waiting for the prices to go down, because the merchants prefer selling their products off at closing time rather than taking them back with them.

Father asks us what we'd like to eat.

"Nothing," we answer in chorus.

Nonetheless, he takes us to an apple stall, buys a few for us, and recommends that we eat them with bread. Then he turns back to take the village road. He's got several hours of walking ahead of him.

Tuesday, December 12

All the comrades say we're going to have a music test this afternoon. I'm suddenly frightened.

The music teacher comes in. The class head shouts, "Everyone up."

The teacher announces, "Sit down. Exam time today."

My heart sinks ever lower. The teacher chooses Tian Yuzhou. He gets up and sings. Then everyone has a turn, one after another. When my turn comes, the teacher asks me to get up.

"Sing."

I start on "Little Rooster Likes His Fight."

"Very good!" she compliments me.

My heart immediately lifts. I'm full of joy. When I go home, I'll have a good grade to show my parents.

Wednesday, December 13

This morning after gym it was time for natural sciences. The teacher came in and immediately said, "Make good use of the fresh air this morning: recite by heart lesson twenty-five, 'The First Snow.'"

We all start to recite.

The teacher explains the text to us. I find him very engaging today. It's the first time all term that I've seen him smile and look relaxed. Yet, when he explains the text, I don't really understand his enthusiasm.

It's only during break that I realize what he meant. He was explaining what goes on in snowy areas. In the text children play in the snow, throw snowballs, make snowmen. I think the teacher must have been thinking of the pleasures of his own childhood. That's why he was so likable today and there was a big smile on his face. Let's hope I'm right.

Saturday, December 16

This morning Father, Mother, my brothers, and I are all sitting on the *kang* watching a series called *Heroic Children*. Just as the first episode is drawing to an end, the second daughter of my second uncle, Huahua, comes running in. She asks me, "Little cousin, do you want to go and watch a funeral?"

I ask my mother if I can go out. She says I may. I change my clothes and put on my shoes.

I go off with Huahua. We walk behind the coffin of an old village woman we barely know. We walk for a long time, and I start to feel I have had enough. But since we've already come a long way, there's no point in turning back. When we get to the end of the procession, in the middle of the fields we hear the weeping of the dead woman's daughters and daughters-in-law. And I start crying too, despite myself.

Monday, December 18
Fine weather

This morning after gym our Chinese teacher advised us to study the first part of our book. "There may very well be a test. Those who work well will be rewarded."

Once again my heart all but stopped beating. I was so anxious, I could barely get a word out.

The best pupils study with a smile on their lips, confidence written on their faces. I and a few comrades, who are perhaps the worst in the class, watch the others study with fear in our hearts. I'm afraid I'm going to stay frozen like this, like the last time, because I have so little faith in myself.

I lower my head. Then I remember that the teacher said that if we studied well, we would certainly do well on the test.

After school the comrades go out to get their meal. I stay behind in class all alone and write. Today, I'm fasting. There are only a few days left until Ramadan is over, and I want to hold out until the end.

When I go back to the dorm, the comrades are busy eating. They discuss things while they chew. I sit down beside them and listen.

Wednesday, December 20

After classes I go back to the dorm to sweep up. I have barely got through half of the room when the head of the dorm, Ma Jing, comes in and starts sweeping as well. I ask her why she's going to this trouble, and she replies that it's to help me.

When we've finished, we sit down on the bed to rest. Ma Xiaohong and my cousin come into the dorm. They're going to wash their hair, they announce. They boil a pot of water and get started. I go out onto the porch to write in my diary. I can hear them talking. They criticize my attitude.

I feel like going in and telling them I can hear what they're saying. But since we've been friends for so many years, I don't.

Why is it that for some time now the people closest to me have been saying bad things about me? What is the answer to this mystery?

This afternoon we have a history test. Our history teacher comes in holding the copies of the test. I haven't yet had time to read my course book and I'm very worried. I fear I'll fail. But when I learn we can use the book in the exam, I'm thrilled.

At this moment I remember a little saying of Mother's and I decide not to open the book. I have to count on my true abilities to cross this hurdle.

After the exam I check my answers against others'. I can hardly believe that mine are exactly the same as theirs.

You have to count on your own strengths truly to succeed.

Tuesday, December 26

This morning Mother prepares dinner and cleans the house. She boils up a pot of water for me so that I can wash my clothes. I pour the water into a tin basin and start my washing. I've only washed two things when a lot of people arrive, among them my grandmother. They talk and laugh so noisily that it feels as if the roof is going to fall in.

I carry on washing my school clothes, and think that it really is at home that things are happiest and that we forget our misfortunes.

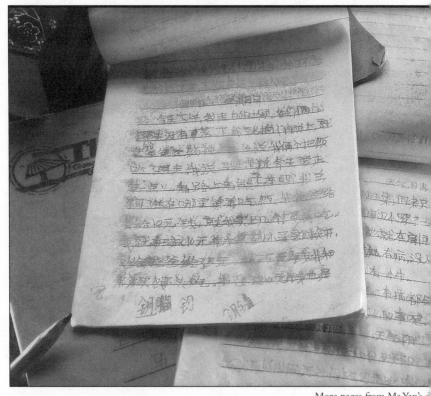

More pages from Ma Yan's d

THE DIARY: PART TWO

Ma Yan's diary starts again on July 3, 2001, after an interruption of six months during which it looked as if she might never return to school. During these six months, she carried on writing in her diary, but it literally went up in smoke. Her father had developed the habit of using his children's old notebooks for cigarette paper. Without knowing that's what he was doing, he had used his daughter's diaries.

At the beginning of July, Ma Yan was preparing to return to her village for the summer break, after having taken the entrance exam for the best school in her area, the girls' senior school in the city of Tongxin.

Yesterday I came back from Tongxin, the largest city in the district. It was the first time I'd been there. If it wasn't for this exam, I might never in my life have had the opportunity of going there and seeing the outside world.

Last night I slept next to my best friends, Ma Zhonghong and Ma Xiaohong. I woke up very early this morning to go to the market to find a tractor from my village. People assured me that a tractor had arrived, but I couldn't find it. So I sat down at the entrance to the market and waited for my father. The vehicle didn't come. Nor did my father. Tears in my eyes, I went back to school to get my bag. I looked for Teacher Chen so that he could open the dorm for me, but unfortunately he wasn't around. I had to get in through the window. I know it's a bad habit, but I had no choice.

By the time I found my bag, the tears were flowing all the way down to my clothes. Other children, too, are leaving for vacation, but their parents are here to carry their things for them. I had to get my luggage out through the window, which is hard enough in itself.

On the street, the sun burns. It's hard to open my eyes. My back is running with sweat, as if it had been drenched with a bucket of water. I don't know whether it's because of the burning sun or because I'm carrying too much luggage.

At the market I finally find a tractor from my village. I put all my things on it and go off once more to look for my father. I don't find him, but I bump into my third uncle. He asks me if I've eaten. When I say no, he invites me to have something to eat a little way farther along the road. We come across two young women. Both of them suggest that we come into their restaurants. We go into one, and right away the other woman starts to swear at us.

The woman whose restaurant we're in points at me and asserts, "This girl eats here often."

I'm very surprised to hear that. I've never eaten there this term. After the meal I feel bad. Is it because she's poor that she has to lie like this? If her business was doing better, she wouldn't have to make up such stories.

Wednesday, July 4

This afternoon my mother and I go and visit my paternal grandparents. When we arrive, my grandfather is sitting on the doorstep. He's watching over my fifth uncle's children.

We ask Grandpa where Grandmother is. He answers that she's in the big cave my uncle dug near his house. I run over there imagining that my grandmother is busy preparing a good meal. Once I'm inside, the first thing I see is her white hair, then her clothes, all soiled. She's turning the hay. I ask her what she's doing. She says the donkey has no food left and she's getting fodder for him.

I lower my head and wonder what use we are in this world. Those who have work can make a contribution toward the country. Those who don't only sleep and eat. My grandmother came into this world some eighty years ago. Why has she never known any happiness in her life? Did she annoy the heavens in some way? Or is her fate just a bad one?

Her mother died five months after she was born. She was raised by her maternal grandmother. Then she married my grandfather and led this difficult life.

Friday, July 13
A fine day

This afternoon, after cutting the wheat, my mother washed her hands and started making the bread we would take with us into the fields tomorrow.

My father is sitting on the threshold. He's rolling cigarettes. I'm off to wash my hair. My two brothers are spreading a plastic sheet outside because it's too hot to sleep indoors. We've been spending nights in the open air.

My mother finishes steaming the bread. She calls my father to the table. I come in after him. I take a bowl of black rice and swallow it down. The bowl empty, I want to get some more, but there's none left. My brother has eaten it all. I ask my mother whether I can have one of her rolls, but she says, "No. It's for tomorrow." She doesn't even let me nibble at a tiny one.

I go outside to sleep. I lie looking up at the stars and think, *Is it because I haven't passed the entrance exam for the girls' senior school that my mother is so angry with me?** I begin to resent her. She won't

---

*Ma Yan has heard through the rumor mill that she hasn't gotten into the school. She will therefore go back to school in Yuwang.

even let me eat my fill before sleeping. My tears start to flow. But I also think she probably has her own reasons for being upset. Why does she take so much trouble over everything? It's always for our studies, so that we can succeed in life, have happy families of our own.

I have to study hard. Even if I haven't got through the entrance exam this time, in three years, I'll do it.

Saturday, July 14
Good weather

This afternoon, just after I've woken from my nap, someone comes to visit. It's the son of one of the village's rich men. His father is called Ma Zhanchuan. The villagers have given him the nickname of Lao Gan, or Old Prune, because he's so dry. His son has come to ask my father if we could cut their wheat for them. My father goes to see them. On his return, I ask him whether we've accepted the job. "Yes," he says.

The whole family goes off to the fields to harvest Ma Zhanchuan's wheat. While we're working, my mother stands tall and says to us, "When we've cut the wheat, I'll give you each ten yuan. You can eat whatever you want at the market."

I literally jump for joy, then I suddenly notice a comrade who passed the entrance exam for the school in Tongxin. My heart sinks down to my knees. I can't take my eyes off the girl. Nor can I see straight. It seems to me the hills and the sky are moving. Mother looks at me and asks what's wrong.

"Nothing," I tell her. "Nothing."

I bend down again. What earthly right do I have to buy good things at the market? I haven't even managed to get into a good senior school. I should be ashamed. I shall have to work really hard not to fail next time and disappoint my parents.

The entire family works in the fields

HARVESTING

Children take part in all the farming work when they're not at school. They help harvest grains, feed the animals, and fetch water from the wells. The Ma family, like most of the poor peasants in the region, depends on human labor, sometimes with the help of a donkey or a small ox. Harvesting is done with a scythe. Only the "rich" have tractors, which cost about six thousand yuan.

Some families supplement their income by harvesting *fa cai*, a hairy grass that grows wild on the steppes of northwest China. In addition to representing this grass, the two characters used to write *fa cai* can also mean "to make one's fortune." "Get rich" is a greeting the Chinese use at the lunar New Year. In the 1990s, this pun lead to *fa cai*'s popularity as garnish for soups and salads in China's cities. Though *fa cai* has no nutritional value, the demand for—and price of—the grass soared.

Peasants travel hundreds of miles to perform the backbreaking work of harvesting the dry black grass, which is a little like algae but as fine as hair. The amount of money they make for this exhausting labor is tiny by the standards of urban China. But it is crucial to families whose annual incomes never exceed a few hundred yuan.

Picking *fa cai* was, however, outlawed by the government in

2000 for environmental reasons. Hundreds of miles of Inner Mongolia have been turned into desert by the pulling up of *fa cai*, and this is thought to contribute to violent sandstorms that hit Beijing each spring and travel as far as Korea and Japan.

The prohibition on harvesting *fa cai* threatens to plunge the poorest peasants—who have no other means of subsistence—into total misery. Neither the threat of being stopped by the police nor the possibility of being attacked by angry Mongolian herdsmen, furious at the plight of their disappearing pastures, has halted the harvest.

As one peasant explained, "Even if we are frightened, we have no choice. We have nothing to eat." For them, *fa cai* doesn't mean getting rich, it simply means survival.

A tractor carrying exhausted peasants who have been picking *fa cai*

This afternoon at four o'clock, after our rest, Mother started to prepare dinner. I helped her to make the fire. After we'd eaten, the whole family went back to the fields to cut more wheat. A little while later, my mother was tying the wheat into bales when she suddenly sat down and got very pale. She moaned softly and said her stomach pains had begun again.

There she is, sitting in the wheat, but we carry on mowing with our sickles.

Tears and the perspiration of pain run down my mother's face. Her eyes are red. Her hands are arched over her stomach. My father tells her to go home. No, she'll wait for us, she says. I lower my head and think, *Why does my mother want to do this harvesting when she is so gravely ill? Why?*

For us, of course. So that we don't have to lead a life like hers.

This morning while we were scything the wheat in the fields, my legs suddenly began to ache horribly. I sat down for a moment.

My mother started in on me. "Really, Ma Yan. You're exaggerating!"

My little brother Ma Yiting rubs it in. "All students exaggerate. Look at our other comrade over there. It takes her half an hour just to get up!"

And my mother adds, "Even if that girl's exaggerating, she's brought honor on her family. She's succeeded in her exam. You . . . you disappoint me too much."

At that moment tears I'm not even aware of start pouring down my cheeks. They won't stop. My mother is always extreme in her comments. She says things, then repeats them, then insists on them. How to bear it all?

I mustn't resent her. At heart I'm only angry at myself. If I had gotten into the girls' school, she wouldn't have spoken such hurtful words. She has her own problems. If she works hard, it's so that we can go to school.

In the village I'm good at a great many things, and few of the children can do better than me. That's why my mother counted on my getting into the best school. But I let her down. How could she not be disappointed in me? She must be very upset.

Saturday, July 28
A fine day

This afternoon around three o'clock my mother is so ill, she can't even get up. My brother and I give her some medicine to ease her pain. We rub her stomach with a cream. We haven't finished when my cousin Ma Yiwu, the son of my father's eldest brother, arrives.

This youth of twenty-five has completed a degree from a technical school, but he's having trouble finding work. He says that work in a successful business is bought with bribes and corruption.

He comes in and sits down at the edge of the bed. He looks bothered. My mother asks him if he's found work. My cousin answers, "It's easy to find work, but you have to pay for it under the table. If I had two thousand yuan, I could get into a company. The problem is money. My family has no money. In a few days I'm going off and will get any old job. When I've earned enough money, then I'll buy myself into a proper position."

I'm sitting on the stool and I notice that his eyes have filled with tears. When I see his hair, already going white, and his tortured face, my heart breaks. Why is it that the children of two generations of soldiers can't find work? Today the grandson of a military hero has a degree, but no money, and as a result can't find a job. Are the heavens blind? Do they only know how to take care of the most wicked people? Are they mocking the lives and deaths of good people? It's all so unjust.

I don't know where my cousin went off to. I hope he'll find a good job soon. It will make me incredibly happy for him.

Monday, July 30
A fair day

This afternoon, when I want to start writing in my diary, I can't find my pen. I ask my brothers. No, they haven't seen it. I look for it in the place where I was doing my writing yesterday, and it isn't there either. I ask my mother. She says that yesterday she noticed that I had left my pen and notebook on the bed and she was worried that they'd get lost, so she put them away in the drawer. But my pen isn't there. I'm distraught.

You're probably going to start laughing. "A pen. What a little thing to get so distressed about!"

If only you knew the trouble I had to take to get that pen. I saved up my pocket money for two weeks. Some of my comrades have two or three pens, but I had none and I couldn't resist buying one.

The difficulties I faced in getting this pen are a mirror of all my other problems. My mother had given me some money with which to buy bread. For days, I had only eaten yellow rice. I preferred going hungry and saving so that I could buy the pen. How I suffered for that pen!

Then I got another pen. I won it at the Children's Day celebrations on the first of June for being a good student. From then on, I no longer lacked pens.

But my dear old pen gave me a sense of power. It made me understand the meaning of a difficult life or a happy life. Every time I see the pen, it's as if I were seeing my mother. It's as if she was encouraging me to work hard and make it into the girls' senior school.

Now I've disappointed my mother. What am I but a useless burden? At school I lead a life that isn't worthwhile. I couldn't make it into the girls' school. What's the use of going on?

But I must think positively. I have to succeed. I will, I really will find an ideal job. And I'll be happy with it.

This morning Mother and Father went off to work in the fields. No one had yet taken them any bread. My brother Ma Yichao said he would go and asked me to cut the grass for the donkey. I took the basket and the scythe and went out. I walked along to my fourth uncle's house and called to my other brother, Ma Yiting, who was there, and we went off together. A few small children followed us. We all worked side by side. We each cut a bagful of grass, then went home laughing and chatting. Everyone looked very happy.

Maybe they think this is the end of their work for the day, that now it's their turn to ask for things. . . . Will they go on living in this ridiculous manner?

I must study hard. When I'm older I'll make sure that my children have happy days, that they're not always caught up in money problems, which is the case at home now. If they don't go to school, I'll ask them to grow grass and tend the ox and the sheep. Then what they earn in a year will be enough to support them.

But I'm already planning my future life even though I have no idea if I'll succeed. Let's hope so.

This afternoon, when my parents got back from their work in the fields, they fell asleep on the bed. I went out to tether the donkey and give him some grass to eat. When I came back inside, I saw that my parents were even more deeply asleep. I didn't wake them. I found a little wood for burning and some dung and brought them in. I took yesterday's ashes out of the stove and started to light the fire. But it wouldn't take. Nothing I did would make it light. I wanted to die.

At that moment I understood how painstaking Mother has to be when she prepares our food. Just getting the fire going is a struggle. I've tried it just once and it makes me want to die. How has Mother managed to keep the fire alight, let alone do all our cooking for so long?

I started helping in the kitchen at the age of seven. Many years have passed since then. I've also lit the fire in the stove on occasion, but always with the help of my brothers. Today I'm alone. But I've got to get it going.

Finally I manage and I can start cooking. When the food is ready I wake my parents so that they can eat. During the meal Mother starts to tell stories from her childhood. It's so nice to listen to her. She laughs, and her eyes seem to laugh at the same time. I want her to laugh all the time and wish she had no more worries and no reasons to be sad.

If only my wish would come true!

Thursday, August 9
A fair day

This morning my two brothers went out to cut grass for the donkey while Father was working on the threshing floor. Mother is ill. She stayed in bed.

I tried to get the fire going for the meal, but my brothers came back before it caught. I asked them why they had been so quick.

"We want to work today. When we've finished eating, Cousin She, a friend from the village, is coming to pick us up so that we can walk to Wangshanwa together and help with the harvest there. It's an hour away."

Soon lunch is ready. Cousin She arrives. I fill two bowls for my parents and also offer one to She. But She doesn't want to eat. So I offer the bowl to my brother. We're sitting on the threshing floor, which has been tidied up, and we laugh and talk. Cousin She tells us a story.

"When we go to pick *fa cai*, we always have a great time. My fifth uncle's grandmother always sings while she's scything. And she dances. All the people at the top of the hill stop working and just watch her. She's such a spectacle. She may be old, they say, but she's got a joyous heart and wonderful character."

I don't believe this description of the grandmother's character. I believe this woman to be sad and unhappy. How do I know? Because my mother's done the same work. So this grandmother who's been cutting grass all her life into her old age, who's never had a decent outfit of clothes, who had to earn money to find a good wife for her son . . . well, now her life is so unenviable that her only joy is dancing. If she doesn't dance now, she'll never have time to dance at all.

Why are we alive? The rich die after having known all kinds of pleasures. It's a happy death. The poor live with tears in their eyes. When they die, their death is painful. And that's the truth of it.

Farming methods have remained traditional and labor intensive in this area.

Saturday, August 11
A fine day

Today at midday I finished eating, then went into the kitchen to wash the pot. My parents and brothers stayed in the room to watch a film on television. I washed up then came back to write in my diary.

Mother is feeling very bad. Always these stomach pains. I write a few words on a scrap of paper that I stick to the door: "Mother is ill. She's resting. Don't go in unless it's urgent. Come back later."

I haven't quite finished writing this, when Mother calls me. She's feeling sick, nauseous. The traditional medicine hasn't helped at all. I come close to her, and she takes my hand and won't let it go. She's still feeling awful. I call Father to come and have a look at her, but he only chides her. Mother cries and laughs at the same time.

I'm terrified. I don't know why Mother has had so many bizarre illnesses these last years. When she's going through a crisis, the whole family is desperate. The worst thing is that when she's ill, the sweat pours down her face like water. I don't know how she can stand it. In her shoes, I think I'd have died of the pain. I really hope she gets better soon.

Sunday, August 12
Fine weather

Tomorrow I have to travel a long distance to harvest *fa cai*. I'm following the road my mother has taken so many times. Now that she's ill, I have to go with my father and my brother, so that we can earn enough to live. And take care of Mother. Then I want to earn a little more money so that I can make my dreams come true. I want to go and study in the district school. But since Mother has been ill, our lives are so hard.

I really don't know why the heavens are treating us like this. Why everything is so unjust.

Monday, August 27

Tonight I'm repairing a wooden box when Mother asks my brother and me to go out and cut a little grass from behind the house for the donkey, who hasn't eaten all day. We go. My brother has only torn off a single handful of grass when he stops to pee.

Ten minutes go by and he still isn't back. I call him and he appears, grumbling, "I can't pull the grass up. I'll have to go and get a scythe." Again he runs off, and I have time to cut almost a bagful of grass.

I call him again, loudly. This time he comes back with a little grass and has the gall to ask me why I'm not cutting any more. I tell him I've finished and it's his turn now.

At home Mother starts snapping at me again. "How long do you expect me to continue being your servant? Since you've come home, you behave like a mandarin." I don't know what she means by the word *mandarin*.

She adds, "You're like my mother, or my grandmother. I serve you. I've raised you. Do you think you have worked as hard? I'm ashamed of you. The daughter of the Yangs is younger than you, yet she passed the entrance exam for the girls' school. And you? You've disappointed me far too much. Tear up all your books.

There's no point in going to school tomorrow. You and your ancestors . . . who are you, after all? Your ancestors begged in order to eat. Even if I finance your studies, what will you be able to do? It would be better if you died right away. Every day I hope that you're going to die. If you die, I'll bury you under a bit of earth and at least I'll be at peace for a few days."

I'm staggered. I don't know why Mother is talking like this. Is she angry or does she really believe what she's saying?

In any case she's wrong. Why doesn't she put herself in my place? Tomorrow I have to leave. And what do I feel? It's hard leaving my family, leaving my mother. My heart isn't light. And when Mother speaks to me like this, tears flood my heart. I can't contradict her. I have to win all the honors, both for my mother and for my ancestors. I want them to be at peace and proud of me, even if they're in the ground.

Tuesday, August 28
A cloudy day

This morning at about six o'clock my father got the cart and donkey ready. He took my brother Ma Yichao and me to Yuwang. School is about to start. It's our first year in the middle school.

When we get there, Father helps take our things out of the cart, then sets off for home. We're alone again.

The bell announces the beginning of classes. I'm in a different one from Ma Yichao, so he heads off in one direction, I in another.

When I get there, the teacher asks me why I'm in class four.

I say, "Maybe it's because I didn't work well enough."

"Why do you say that? This year is different from last, when the best students were in classes one, two, and three. This year the classes aren't streamed according to your level. I hope you're not getting discouraged."

I take in what the teacher says and store it up inside me.

Having told me to sit down, he's gone out of the room.

The comrades are making a lot of noise, like mice fighting once the cat has left. My head feels completely empty, except for the noise around me. These boys and girls are all a little bigger than me. They swear all the time and they don't look like middle school students. Our class has seventy students in it. Imagine what it's like when everyone speaks at the same time. How is one to work in here?

I'm so upset. What I hate most about myself is the fact that I cry so easily. I don't want to cry now, but I can't seem to stop myself.

THE MIDDLE SCHOOL IN YUWANG

The middle school in Yuwang has more than one thousand pupils. It consists of a series of enormous redbrick buildings. The benches are makeshift. There is a single blackboard. Plaster peels from walls unpainted for years. In a school such as this, the task of teaching is formidable, as is that of learning. Yet the students work hard, and many desire to take their studies further and attend college.

Boarders provide their own rice. Twice a year, at the beginning of the term, each pupil has to bring a fifty-five-pound sack of rice to school. Every day the rice is prepared in large cauldrons by women who do the cooking for the whole school. Just as in the last school, one of the school buildings is a kitchen, where students go to fetch their meals, which they take back to the dormitory to eat on their beds. There are sixteen girls in Ma Yan's dormitory, all of them from the surrounding villages. The beds are crowded against each other, but the girls don't complain.

Each pupil gets a bowl of rice for lunch. If they want an extra spoonful of vegetables, usually potatoes, they have to pay an additional ten fen. There's never any meat. There are no other meals, neither breakfast nor dinner.

Ma Yan has no money for vegetables. She eats a bit of steamed roll at dinner, which her mother has made and which she keeps in a box. Only when she goes home for the weekends can she hope to satisfy her hunger.

The Yuwang middle school

After school I meet two comrades who were in my class in the elementary school. They haven't gone home because we have a study period in the evenings, and their families live far away. Their results are a little worse than mine, one or two points lower. But they're in classes one or two. I'm too depressed to talk to them.

Other friends come and play. They look happy. I think of my two best friends from elementary school. But they've left school now. I'm all alone. Their families are better off than mine, but they don't want to go to school anymore. I don't understand them.

The study hour arrives. The English teacher asks me to go to class three. The teacher there tells me I'm in his group. I find all this very strange.

Monday, September 3

This afternoon my old elementary-school friends Ma Shaolian and Bai Xue come to my dorm. They're not boarders. I'm very happy to see them again; it's as if we were back in elementary school. They look as pretty and happy as ever.

We sit down to talk. Without knowing why, I turn my head to the right. I see a comrade taking a schoolbook down and starting to read. My friends say, "What on earth is she studying now? All the teachers like her."

I think to myself, *Here's this girl who's already a good student, but she carries on working while I sit around doing nothing at all. That can't be right.*

I say good-bye to my friends and go back to my books. I really have to work hard so that I can eventually get that ideal job and have Mother stop worrying about me.

Tuesday, September 4
A fine day

In the last class today there's a general cleanup of the school.

The term is starting. All the comrades are happy. We've finally arrived at the portal of secondary education. We have a lot of enthusiasm, a lot of goodwill. We put a lot of energy into our work.

Our teacher asks us to clean the area behind the school. He's like an old hen taking a group of chicks off to feed. The comrades make clucking sounds and clean with vigor. In very little time, the work is done. The teacher tells us to go off and rest.

All the comrades have gone, and I'm standing alone on the sports field, watching the others at work. This school must have a thousand pupils. They work hard. If there were more like them, we'd certainly be able to plant more trees for China.* How wonderful it would be if there were more of us.

---

*The government has started a program to grow trees.

Thursday, September 6
A fine day

Today after school some parents came to collect their children. They went off together to eat good things in the market. My brother and I haven't eaten for two days. We only have hard old black bread to chew on. So we go off to the market to look for our parents. But they haven't come. I think that Mother is probably not at home. When we left last week, she said she was going to go off to pick *fa cai* on Monday or Tuesday.

I think so often of Mother! I don't know how long it will be until I see her again. I want to see her hands, her poor hands.

Friday, September 7
A dull day

This morning our last lesson is politics. A very tall teacher comes in. He's about twenty-seven and exceedingly handsome. He must be a Han, while all my other teachers are Hui. The Hans' pronunciation is very different from that of Huis, very rigid. We don't understand everything they say. I only grasped a single whole phrase: "Make progress in your studies."

Why do all the teachers repeat this? It makes us feel we're under constant pressure. But I'm going to do my best. I'll achieve my goals.

Ma Yan in her dormitory

After school a few of the comrades with money were allowed to leave early. They got onto a tractor for a yuan. Only my little brother and I are walking. On the track, the sun burns down on us, and we think we'll die of thirst. My brother asks an old man for a watermelon. We both crouch at the side of the road and eat, like dogs who've been chased out of the house. We really look pitiful.

When we get home, the yard is empty. I know Mother has

116

gone. My paternal grandfather comes out of the house and says, "Ah, my little grandchildren are home. Come, you must be very hungry."

My brother says that there's a watermelon in the wooden school box. I cut it and share it with my grandfather. While I eat, I think of my mother. I don't even know how she is. Her stomach was bad again. And picking *fa cai* is such hard work. Really hard. Especially if you're ill.

When will I be able to keep Mother from exhausting herself for us like this? I really want her to have a better life. One in which she doesn't have to go so far away to work. One in which she won't suffer. I just hope my wish comes true.

Sunday, September 9
A somber day

This afternoon my paternal grandmother came to visit. It's as if my mother had come home. I gave her a slice of watermelon. I was writing in my diary at the table.

While she eats, my grandmother says to me, "You look so serious! I really wonder what it is you're writing. Our lives have so little interest."

"Don't say that, Grandmother," I reply. "I'll read you what I'm writing."

While I read, tears flow down my grandmother's face.

"We old ones," she says to me, "we're good for nothing. And it's because of us that you suffer."

"Oh no, Grandmother. Don't talk like that. It's because of you

117

that I've been able to live until now. Without you, I wouldn't have understood anything about life."

I think, then, of some things my mother keeps repeating: "No matter all our problems and exhaustion, I'm going to pay for your studies so that you become people of talent, so that you make a contribution to the country, so that you don't live a life like mine, which has no interest or value in it."

I won't disappoint my mother. She'll see what kind of daughter she has.

Monday, September 10
A fine day

It's market day again today. I have to go back to school, this school that I can't leave. But since today is Teachers' Day, we have a holiday.

When I get down from the tractor, the driver asks me for money. But I don't have any. I tell him I'll pay him the next time. But he won't let me go. I take out my pen and offer it to him. He refuses. This time it's he who says I can pay him on the next journey.

When I go through the school gates, I'm crying without knowing why. Maybe because I'm thinking of Mother. I don't know how she's getting on up in the mountains, but I know how tough life is there.

Every time I'm faced with a difficulty, I think of my mother.

What I told the driver was a lie. The teachers say students shouldn't lie. They should be honest. But I had no choice. I asked my father for money, and he told me we had no money; don't I know the problems the family is facing?

I stopped asking him for money then. If I had gone on, he would have gotten angry.

Had I explained all that to the driver, he would have made fun of me, and especially of my father. He would have condemned him and thought, *What a father, a good-for-nothing. He can't even pay for a tractor ride for his child!*

My father does his best. And I don't want anyone saying bad things about him. That's why I lied.

Wednesday, September 12
A fine day

This evening during study time, the English teacher comes in and asks, "Do you really want to learn English?"

We shout a unanimous, "Yes."

He goes on, "Since you really want to learn English well, I suggest you each contribute one yuan, and we'll be able to buy a tape recorder so that you can work on your own during study hours in the evening. How about it?"

The comrades agree.

The teacher goes on, "Do any of you have financial problems?"

"No," they all reply in chorus.

He adds, "If anyone has a money problem, put your hand up."

I put my hand up.

The teacher asks, "Does your family have problems?"

I answer him in English, "Yes."

Since he's the English teacher, I'm supposed to speak to him in English.

He says, "If you really have financial problems, you won't have to contribute. Some families are in real difficulty. They can't even pay their children's school fees."

I think of my third year of primary school. I had no money to buy schoolbooks. Mother and a few women she knows went off to pick *fa cai*. With that money, I could buy my own books. But I missed a few months of school. At the beginning I understood nothing at all. Then, after two or three months of hard work, I caught up.

I feel like shouting at the top of my lungs, My mother is excessively kind to her children. There is nothing she won't do for them. Instead I will write it down. "Mother, you are great. I love you. I love your spirit. You are so strong. So pure. You're an example to your daughter. In your daughter's heart you will always be a great woman."

Thursday, September 13
A fine day

This evening during study hours I look up and notice that I'm all alone in the room. It looks bigger than usual. Suddenly I'm frightened. I grab my bag and fly from the room like a gust of wind.

Outside I meet my friend Yang Yuehua. She's walking very slowly. It seems strange. Usually she's so open and friendly. What's wrong with her today? I ask her what's going on.

It seems her test went very badly. She cries, and I console her.

"It's only a little test. You'll have lots of opportunities to do better. . . ."

She replies through her tears, "My mother has worked so hard for me. And this is the way I pay her back. I can't even thank her properly for all those rolls she makes for me every week."

I'm full of admiration for her. She thinks clearly. Surely she'll study well and have a good career.

Friday, September 14
A gray day

This morning after classes I went to get a bowl of rice. My comrade, Ma Yongmei, went to get water. When we had finished the rice, I put my hand into the very back of the wooden bread box that I keep on my bed, but the bread had all gone long ago. I'm still hungry, because between the two of us, we've only had a half pound of rice.

You're probably going to say, half a pound for two, isn't that enough? But a half pound only fills a small bowl. We shared it. Each of us was only allowed half. If you think that fills us up . . . On top of it, we've run out of rolls.

I watch the others who are eating watermelon, my mouth watering in spite of myself. I've had a cold for a few days and I feel quite sick. I sit dumbly on the edge of my bed. A comrade sees my state and gives me a pill. I feel better after that. That medicine is more precious to me than treasure. This girl is called Bai Jing, and her image is now engraved on my soul. She's someone one can take as a model.

Saturday, September 15
A gray day

Today is the beginning of the weekend. My brother and I walk along the endless path. From the road we can see fields full of melons. We're very hungry. My brother goes off into the fields to steal a little onion, a few turnips, and we eat them on our way. I know that stealing is wrong and that students shouldn't do such things. But what are we to do? If we don't steal from the fields, we probably won't make it home.

I walk slowly. My legs hurt a lot. I think I'm the unhappiest girl in the whole world.

I think of my mother again. I don't know how she is. She gets up at five thirty in the morning and works till seven in the evening. Every day she and the other women who have gone to pick *fa cai* walk with their eyes on the ground, their backs bent to the sky. How many mountains has she scaled this way?

Sunday, September 16
A little rain

Today I have to go back to school. Father has got our things ready for us and given us enough money to get a tractor ride to Yuwang. We climb up on the back wagon. A little farther on, the granddaughter of our third paternal great-uncle* joins us. My second uncle then climbs up onto the tractor. He puts his niece on his lap, and fearing that she may get cold, he wraps a bag over

---

*One of Ma Shunji's younger brothers from the family that adopted him.

her legs. She's already thirteen. Doesn't she know how to take care of herself?

I see them laugh. I also see my little brother shivering from cold. I give him my hat. On this rainy morning, my anger reaches the boiling point.

My paternal grandfather was adopted. He's not really close to these people, who look down on him. My mother won't tolerate any contempt for our generation. She wants us to become people of substance. The trouble my parents take on our account is enormous. When I see the looks these people give us, I think of my grandfather. It's for him that we need to study, so that people look up to us for the rest of our lives.

The long, empty road between school and home

Last night, during the study hour, we had an English test. I found it easy. In less than half an hour I'd finished. The teacher in charge asked us to give him our papers when we had finished. He lectured me, "At that speed, how can you possibly have done well?"

I gave him my paper nonetheless.

But this morning the comrades are all abuzz. They're all saying, "Ma Yan may work well, but she didn't come in first!"

As I listen to them, I'm ashamed. My parents have done so much for me, and this is the way I repay them.

Then I reminded myself that there are more exams to come, at midterm and at the end of term. By then I'll have made great progress. I'll work really hard, with no slacking. I just hope my wishes come true.

Tuesday, September 18
Rain

When our last class is over, our English teacher asks us to stay for another twenty minutes to copy out words. After that we go to get our food, but there's nothing left. There are a few teachers in the canteen too, so I deliberately protest in a loud voice.

"Our stomachs are crying out with hunger. We've run here as quickly as we could, and there's nothing left. We pupils, we dream of nothing but these bowls of rice from morning until evening. How do you expect us to make it through the day? If there were some bread at least . . . But there's no bread. And on top of it all, it's a rainy day! Our spirits grow weaker and weaker, especially on empty stomachs."

The teachers say nothing. How I want to go home and eat my fill. I'll come back to school only when my stomach's full.

Then I remind myself that to study well, you probably have to put up with some suffering.

Thursday, September 20
A gray day

At noon I came back from the canteen with some rice. I put the bowl on the bed. Ma Yongmei divided the rice in two and took her share.

Before I can start on my bowl, my little brother Ma Yichao arrives. He asks, "Sister, have you still got tickets for the canteen? I want to buy some rice."

I borrow a ticket and give it to him.

Then he asks me if I've eaten.

"Yes, I have."

But he guesses that it isn't true.

"You haven't eaten. Your lips are dry. The lips of people who have eaten are moist."

A little while later he comes back and returns the canteen ticket. He says there's no more rice. He goes off again.

How can I help him? I have no money, no bread. I don't know what to do. . . . Yet I'm his older sister and if I have no sense of responsibility, what am I good for? I cry. I tell myself it's not all my fault that our family's financial situation is so dire.

It's impossible to describe the sensation of HUNGER.

Sunday, September 30
A bright day

This afternoon we come back from the grain fields and I'm so hungry, I think I can see smoke coming out of my stomach. As soon as Mother arrives, she goes to the kitchen to prepare food. I ask my father for a yuan so that I can buy an English notebook. One of my cousins, the son of my fourth uncle, comes to visit. He tells me that my mother has lent my fourth-grade books to other children in the elementary school. I ask her if this is true, and she says yes.

I'm angry because those books are still useful to me. How could she have given them away so easily? I want to be able to study. There are questions I still don't understand.

For some time now, when the teacher is lecturing, I haven't been seeing clearly. He'll say for example that this is an even number and this is an odd number, but I can't clearly distinguish what he's writing on the blackboard. Nor can I hear properly. I have to pay close attention to what the teachers and pupils are saying. When you're nearsighted, it's hard to follow the work. If you don't see properly, you can only count on your ears. And when your ears are also bad, then . . .

Mother grumbles at me. "You work so hard, but what have you managed to achieve? Not even the girls' school. What's the point of carrying on? It would be better if you gave it up and came home."

Her criticisms are never-ending. I can't sum them up in a single line. I store up what she says inside myself. I know I'll never forget it.

It's not only her fault. It's mine too. I've disappointed my mother.

My whole family resents me. I feel horribly alone. I think about school life. Keeping up with work is so hard when you can't see. So I think of giving up and coming home. But if this is how my family treats me ... I no longer know what path to take. Who'll show me a good and generous road?

*Tuesday, October 2**
A fine day

When we finish our homework this afternoon, my brother and I go off to our grandmother's, where our father is working for our fifth uncle. As soon as we get there, we help our father move a pile of earth. But when we want to go home again, he asks us to stay a little longer.

Our grandfather starts to tell stories about his youth, dating from his time in the army.

There was one soldier who always wet his bed at night. The head of the squad beat him daily on account of this, but he couldn't seem to rid himself of his bad habit. The other soldiers wanted to stop the beatings, but they couldn't convince their chief. He just wouldn't listen. Worst of all, he tied the feet of the poor youth and hit him so much that he wept. At the end of it all, the soldier was sent home.

Our grandfather confesses that he loathed the head of their squad. But he doesn't tell us anything of his own plight or bitterness. I think he was a great soldier. He won battles and he founded our family, which is a large one. I'm proud of him.

---

*Ma Yan has the week off in celebration of the national holiday.

Grandfather, I want to note it here, how very much I admire you, what a great and brave man I think you are. Throughout the world, from now on, it'll be recognized that you are one of the seeds of our army.

Wednesday, October 3
A fine day

This afternoon my brother Ma Yichao and I did the housework. Then we went to my fifth uncle's, where my father has been working the last few days in order to earn some money. We helped him as best we could.

When I looked at the clock, it was already five. I called my brother because we needed to go back and do our homework.

My fifth uncle's youngest son clung to our legs and whimpered. He wanted to come with us and see his mother. But I knew she wasn't there. She'd gone far away to harvest *fa cai*. His father wasn't there either, and his two elder brothers had gone to stay with their maternal grandmother. I lifted him up in my arms, and he started crying for real.

Seeing his tears, I was reminded of our childhood. When our parents weren't at home, we were pitiable creatures. I carried him to our house and asked myself why, when a child cries or is alone, he always shouts for Mother. Why doesn't he ask for Father?

Market day today. Mother comes home from my maternal grand-mother's. I go out to welcome her on the front porch. My mother's face is as black as coal, and her lips are all cracked. She looks terrible. What's wrong with her? Usually when she comes back from her mother's, she's happy, full of chat and laughter. But today . . .

Mother comes into the room and pours out all her resentments to us. "When someone's poor, it's no good going back to your parents' family. Your grandfather loves me, yet since I left home, he's turned his back on me. He didn't ask me a single question, not even why I had come, or if it was cold on the way. He didn't say a single word.

"I'm really furious. I'm not going to go and see them anymore. Listen to me, all three of you. Study well in order not to grow up like your father, who has suffered the contempt of everyone around him all his life long. Forget the mocking laughter of your maternal grandfather. You'll have to be successful and show him how wrong he's been about everything."

This afternoon I got bored. I called a few children over to play with me. We drew a round circle on the ground in the yard and ran about inside it. Suddenly my paternal grandfather arrived. He had come to eat watermelon. He had a little smile on his face, and I accompanied him into the room and asked him to sit on the *kang*. I placed the low table on the *kang* and cut him a piece of watermelon and another of sweet melon. I handed the slices to him.

Crouched beside him, I watched him. He talked to me while he ate. He's already eighty and he doesn't have much time left. Wouldn't it be wonderful if he could live to be a hundred? By then, even if I haven't got a brilliant career, I'll certainly have some kind of job. And I'll be able to offer him a few last good days.

The sixth lesson of the day is devoted to a daily class meeting. Here's what our main teacher, the one who teaches Chinese, taught us.

The first thing to respect, he told us, is school discipline. The second is our daily ten minutes of morning exercise. Thirdly, our studies: "Those who have greater difficulty than others must start their work earlier and keep to a rigorous schedule, so that they know exactly when it's time to study math and so on. Never think you're behind the others; just get on with it. You can always make progress by studying well."

Why does each teacher talk about making progress? Now every time I think of the word, my hair stands on end. Do you know why? Because in the last English exam, I came in second. It's cruel when I think of it.

But I've taken in what the teacher said today. I have to make a greater effort.

Thursday, October 11
A fine day

This morning after our last class I stay behind to do an essay. Suddenly the head of games comes in and tells me to go outside and join the ranks. "All the others are already lined up. There's only you left."

I go out to the sports ground and concentrate on standing very straight.

The other comrades have just started their games. Some are skipping rope, others are playing soccer, and still others are engaged in a game of tag between an eagle and chickens. I'd like to play too, but my heart isn't in it.

When I hear the children who aren't boarders talking about their families, I automatically think of my own. It makes me want to go straight home to see my mother and to ask her to make me a lovely dish of food. That would be great. I can already see myself chatting away happily to Mother.

Suddenly Ma Yichao runs past me, as fast as the wind. As soon as I see him, I stop having these dark thoughts and go off to play with the others.

I don't know what's wrong with me these days. I'm all upset

about things. I don't know quite what I'm doing or thinking. My moods go up and down.

We have a free period this afternoon. Our English teacher dictates a text to us. Two of the comrades can't manage to write it down. The teacher hits them very hard with the leg of a chair. Bruises immediately appear on their arms and legs.

This teacher wants us to do well, but he hits too hard. I think he enjoys it. I weep without showing the tears. I think their parents would be weeping too, if they saw how badly their children were treated.

The teacher is raging and shouts, "If you still haven't learned your lessons by the next period, I won't give you another chance. I'll choose only the brightest students to answer questions. And that'll be that. I won't come back to you at all."

During the class the teacher calls on me several times. My comrades look at me with envious eyes. They would do anything to get the better of me.

I mustn't worry about this. I mustn't let anything prevent me from attaining my goals and making good my plans for the future. I'll try to do something to change their jealous glances into admiring ones. I'll be as strong as my mother. When she encounters difficulties, she confronts them alone, and no one dares laugh at her.

Failure is the mother of success. But it worries me to see the teacher striking the pupils. What will happen if they get hurt?

During the evening study period, these comrades managed to learn the words they hadn't known before. Why do they work better after they've been beaten? Their parents hope they'll become accomplished people, but after so many difficult years of study, how will they fulfill these expectations?

A skinny dog no longer manages to jump over a wall, even with help.

That's one of my mother's proverbs. I've never forgotten it. But it's only now that I grasp its full meaning.

Thursday, October 18
A fine day

Today in Chinese class the teacher asks us to write an essay on the theme of being in middle school. He takes the opportunity to explain to us the difference between the fast and the slower classes. The worst students in the fast class will be put into the slower class, and the teacher will be punished. That's why he wants us to work hard. All of us will reap the benefits. Finally he stops talking and tells us to start writing.

I finish my essay in a few minutes. All the comrades are surprised. "We take two or three days to think over an essay, and you . . . you just dash one off."

The teacher points out that even this isn't quick enough. "You have to be like Ye Shengtao,* and practice speed and skill."

The comrades make fun of me. "Ye Shengtao is the cleverest

* A famous twentieth-century philosopher.

133

Ma Yan between classes at school

man under the sun. Ma Yan comes in second."

Everyone laughs.

To tell the truth, there's nothing I'd like better than to be the second-cleverest person in the world. If I had the chance, I'd like to compete with grandfather Ye Shengtao. Who knows if my wish might come true?

Today my father has come to town for the market. He waits for me by the door while I'm still busy in class. I'm happy because that means he probably has some money for me. Otherwise he wouldn't wait.

As soon as classes are over, I rush out to meet him. He gives me five yuan, which I'll have to give to the teacher for books. My father asks me if I've run out of bread.

I explain to him that the steamed bread is long finished. He buys two rolls, one for my brother and one for me. I hold on to mine. It's precious. I'll eat it tomorrow on the long road home.

When I get to the vegetable part of the market, I meet comrade Ma Yongmei. I borrowed a roll from her not long ago. She asks me to return what I owe her. I give her the bread rolls I'm holding. But she doesn't want that. She wants money. Where am I going to find money?

Friday, October 26
A fine day

My father gave us four yuan and told my brother and me to get a ride home on a tractor today. My parents are going off to pick *fa cai* again and they were worrying about our safety.

But how in good conscience can I squander money on a tractor ride? My parents are working so hard, breaking their backs, bent over all the time, their faces fixed on the yellow earth. How can we possibly allow ourselves the extravagance of a tractor ride that is paid for with our parents' sweat? My brother and I prefer to walk home.

We set out at eleven in the morning, and it is almost five when we finally reach home. We push open the door. Everything is quiet. The yard is empty. There's no one. No one here to say, "Oh, at last. Here are my exhausted children. Quick. You must rest. Mother is going to prepare a meal for you. . . ."

How I would love to hear Mother's voice. But Mother isn't here.

When it got dark, my brother went off to ask our paternal grandmother if she would keep us company. She didn't come and there's only us, my two brothers and me. We go to sleep silently on the *kang*. Outside everything is quiet, and we're very frightened. If Mother were here, I don't know what she would be talking about. It would probably be one of her funny stories. But she isn't here.

Even cuddled up in bed, we feel the cold. I don't know how Mother manages to sleep on the damp earth—especially since she's ill. What a terrible life she has. How much longer will she have to live this way? I so very much hope she'll soon be happy.

This morning I help my brother Ma Yichao do his English homework. He doesn't even know how to write the simplest words. I get angry and I can't prevent myself from giving him a slap. He starts to cry and doesn't want to go on. Suddenly I start to cry too. . . .

Mother is always lecturing me: "You have to take care of your little brother. You're bigger than he is and have a duty to help him. I send you to school and pay no attention to the costs. If you don't work well, not only do you not deserve the trouble I take for you, but you don't even deserve a week's bread."

Her words play over and over in my mind. But my little brother doesn't work hard. I don't want to have to hear that he's been put into the slow class.

While the two of us are crying, my second uncle comes to the house. He says that an official is busy inspecting one of our pieces of land. "You should prepare this land for planting trees on," he says to us. "Aren't your parents here? Go and see your paternal grandmother then, and ask your fifth uncle to come and dig some holes for the trees." Then he goes away.

What are we to do? Should I be going back to school or staying at home to attend to all this? I'm so confused, I can't even describe it.

And my mother isn't here. . . . Every time I think of her, I want to cry.

Good news today. On Wednesday we're going to have our midterm exam. I'm very happy about it. I fully intend to demonstrate my abilities. I'm no worse than anyone else, apart from the fact that I eat and dress less well than they do. Some girls change their school clothes often. But I've only got one outfit, a pair of trousers and a white shirt, which I have to wash on Saturdays so that they're clean by Monday.

But what does it matter! I only want to study and pay tribute to my parents' hands.* Despite the cold, they're working far away from home for us. Why? For our future. And I mustn't disappoint them.

Tuesday, October 30
A somber day

It's freezing today. My brother and I have no more bread. At lunchtime the comrades are all eating, and we have to stand by and grit our teeth.

Seeing my tears, my brother says, as if his heart were light, "Wait, sister, I'm going to borrow some lunch tickets." But I know he feels no better than I do. He simply wants to console me and stop me from worrying about him. I go back to my dorm and sit on my bed and wait for him to return.

I'm dreaming of this bowl of yellow rice.

---

*A common Chinese expression of gratitude.

He takes a very long time to come back. Then he says, "Sister, there's no more rice."

He turns to leave. I watch my brother's receding back, and I can't help letting the tears flow.

Do you know what hunger is? It's an unbearable pain.

I wonder when I'll stop experiencing hunger at school. . . .

Friday, November 2
Wind

All these last days we've been doing our midterm exams. I think of nothing else, not even my sick mother, who's working so far away.

For the exams some of the comrades have torn out pages of their books and hidden them in their pockets. They'll be punished. Others write answers to difficult questions down the length of their arms. Do you think that's fair?

I haven't even opened my book. I remember that in elementary school a teacher explained to us that before an exam there's no point rereading all your notes. It's better to relax, have fun. "That's the best way to get good results," he said.

I haven't altogether followed his advice. Instead, I sat on the edge of my bed and thought of my parents' suffering.

I can't disappoint them. I *will* do well.

The weekend starts today, and I'm full of joy. I hope that my parents have come home. I'll tell them all about the midterm exams.

I'm busy planning all kinds of projects when a comrade whispers, "The politics teacher knows our exam results."

But another comrade is furious. "He doesn't. He only knows how the best students did, not the results of the dunces like us who aren't ranked among the top students."

I hurry over to the teacher's house. It's already full of students. I've only just come in when I hear the teacher's voice. "Ma Yan got one hundred fourteen points in math. She's come in at the top of all six classes. She got ninety points in Chinese. . . . The English results haven't come in yet."

I'm so overjoyed, I burst into tears. I don't know where so many tears can come from. My vision is blurred, but I go outside again.

I'm so moved, I still can't even find words to describe how I feel. Never have I had a moment like this one. Never will I forget it.

At the class meeting the teacher pinned up our exam results. He explained working methods to us.

"When you're asked to put the answer to a question between parentheses, you don't need to show us the working out of the whole problem."

I know that that's directed at me. He goes on.

"For multiple-choice questions, just choose one answer. There's no point checking two or more answers. Some students often do this. I hope you won't make these same mistakes next time around. For calculations, use the shortest method. To do an analysis, you must read the question carefully and think. . . ."

When he's finished with these explanations, he asks the students to give him the results of each exam, as well as the total, since he needs to fill out a form.

At the end of the day, I have a total of 299 points. I come in second. Someone who is repeating the year comes in first. Tears of joy pour from my eyes. The teacher congratulates me and says everyone should take me as a model.

But the more he talks, the sadder I become, because Mother has had to go far off to work. Everything the teacher said today will stay etched on my mind. If I follow his advice, I think I'll be able to overcome my difficulties.

Next time I will try to come in first.

Tuesday, November 6
A dull day

During class today the politics teacher compliments me once more. He admits that up until now he had paid no attention to me, noticing neither my qualities nor my faults.

"In her midterm exams, comrade Ma Yan has shown lots of potential—potential I hadn't suspected she had. I judged her wrongly. I have already told her what I think of her work. If you

141

Ma Yan in class

don't believe me, ask her. You should know that a comrade of ours wrote in a composition, 'When we hadn't done well on a test, the teacher insulted us, complaining that he had taught a class of idiots and all in vain.' This same girl went on to say, 'Teacher, you shouldn't underestimate us: failure is the mother of success.' This is both a piece of advice she offers to your teacher and the expression of her own feelings. This girl is in our class."

Everyone is staring at me. It's true, I wrote those words. If I did well in these exams, it's largely because of what this teacher said. If he hadn't called us idiots, I would certainly not have gone on to get the results I did.

Wednesday, November 7
A fine day

I'm so hungry, I could eat anything. Anything at all.

When I talk about hunger, I instantly think of my mother. I don't know if she's gotten home safely. Me, I'm happy enough coming to school every day and being hungry. But Mother has to run up mountain slopes every day. And I don't know how she's faring. On top of it all, she's ill.

It's three weeks since I've seen her. I think of her all the time.

I'm terribly hungry. There's been no bread or vegetables since Tuesday. When I eat my rice now, there's nothing to go with it.

I even took some food from a comrade's bowl without asking her. When she came back to the dormitory, she called me all kinds of names.

What can I say to her? When I hear her sounding off, I think of my father, who left my brother and me four yuan. We've been living on that for three weeks, and I still have one left over in my pocket. My stomach is all twisted up with hunger, but I don't want to spend that yuan on anything so frivolous as food. Because it's money my parents earned with their sweat and blood.

I have to study well so that I won't ever again be tortured by hunger and lack of money. When I have a job, I'll guarantee some happy times for my parents. I'll never let them go far away to work for us again.

It's market day. In the English class I'm sitting next to the window. Suddenly I see a shadow from the corner of my eyes. I lift my head. I see Mother behind the window. I'm staggered. It's been so long since I've seen her. Even through the window I can see that her face is all black and swollen.

The class comes to an end without my noticing. In any case, I've taken nothing in. It's not important. I'll ask the teacher what I've missed at the next lesson. First I have to find Mother.

Father and Mother are waiting for me in the street. I'm so happy! It's so long since we've all been together. Father, Mother, my brother, and me. We walk down the street, all together. We talk about all kinds of things and forget about our stomachs. Suddenly Mother taps her forehead. "But you two, you haven't eaten yet?"

We shake our heads.

She takes us to the market. She buys us vegetable soup for fifty fen and we also get bread to dunk in the bowl.

After we've eaten, we go off to buy winter clothes. With good padded clothes, we won't be cold. We each get a jacket and shoes and socks. In no time at all we've spent over a hundred yuan. What a pity! I feel both happy and sad. Money is so hard to earn and so easy to spend. You don't even notice it going.

I don't know how Mother and Father have earned these hundred yuan, how many days it took, how many tens of hours, hundreds of minutes, thousands and thousands of seconds. And I spent all this hard-earned wealth as if it were nothing at all.

When I grow up, what won't I do for my parents!

Friday, November 9
A nice day

Tomorrow we go home, and I'm so happy.

Tonight during the study hour there was a blackout. All the comrades were thrilled. They were happy not to have electricity to see by: a whole hour in which to have fun.

But I'm happy just to go home, to sit down with my mother and talk things over.

Several weeks have passed since we were all together at home. This time when we get there, I'm going to ask my parents how they spent every single day, and especially how Mother's health is. I think her pains started again when she was up in the mountains.

Sunday, November 11
A fine day

This morning at about five o'clock, Mother got up to prepare our food, worried that we would be hungry. Then she woke us. We got dressed, washed, and sat down to breakfast.

While I ate, I noticed that my mother's eyes, face, feet, and hands were all swollen. I asked her what was wrong, and she said, "Nothing, nothing. Maybe I got up too quickly. . . ."

I know that's not the reason. Her attacks are bad again.

I ask her if the swelling is caused by her illness.

"What illness?" She stares at me. "I must have woken you up too early. You're still all mixed up. Eat. Quickly . . ."

A vehicle pulls up, and my mother makes it an excuse to put an end to my questions. I know she's running away from them, just so that I don't worry about her.

I will study well. Otherwise I won't deserve Mother's hard-working hands that have prepared our breakfast this morning.

Monday, November 12
A fine day

What I really want is to go home, straightaway, without waiting for the weekend. I want to see Mother's face and her hands again. Because I know that she's going away to work again. Far away . . . I don't want her to go away, but I don't know how to prevent it.

Last week when we got home, Mother wanted to see my report card. I showed her my test results. After she had looked at them, she smiled.

"I haven't spent all this money for nothing," she concluded. "You haven't disappointed my expectations in the least."

She looked at my brother's results too and she exploded. "How can you possibly think you deserve the bread you take away with you every week? How do you think I managed to get through the exhaustion of the mountains? My hope in you, that's how. And now look at the results! How can I help but be disappointed. And sad."

When I think of my mother, I really want to go home. I feel

like asking for permission to leave. But even if I go home, I fear I may already have missed her. She's probably left already to harvest *fa cai*. I can only wish her good health. Because if her illness starts again, there's no one there to look after her. This time Father isn't going with her. He's staying at home to take care of the house and the fields.

How I hope that her attacks don't start again. She only had a two- or three-day break at home before setting off again to try and earn some more money. How I love it when we're all together as a family, eating and talking. I really want to have a warm and happy family! But the heavens don't seem to want it, and they force me to live in melancholy and pain.

But the unhappiest person of all is Mother. All year long she has to leave home to work far away. That's where her illness came from. From going off to earn money to support the three of us children. And my brother hasn't brought honors home from school. So of course she's sad.

I have to carry on working hard so that I don't disappoint her. The biggest wishes in my life are that she gets better and that our family is at last together for good.

If ever I succeed in life, my success will equally be Mother's. I'll always remember her.

Why am I always so unhappy; why do my tears never dry? Tell me why? Will I only succeed when I have no tears left? And if they don't dry up, is that a sign that I won't ever succeed?

I must persist on this difficult path.

I don't know where Mother spent last night, whether she slept on the damp ground or on a rocky promontory at the edge of a road. I'm only certain of one thing. I know she didn't sleep well. The temperature has gone right down to below zero. On top of that, there are her stomach problems.

I know how hard it is to pick *fa cai*. I did it once with my father. It was still summer. At one in the morning, the tractor we were on ran out of fuel. We had to get off and sleep in a field on the bare ground. In no time at all, I was covered with dust. It crawled up my nostrils. I breathed it. I couldn't get to sleep. I sat up and counted the stars in the sky.

I thought of a story we'd once had to read called "The Child Who Counts the Stars." Once upon a time there was a boy who leaned against his grandmother at night and counted the stars. His grandmother told him the stars were beyond number, uncountable. But the boy answered that, provided he believed he could, he would somehow manage to count them.

I didn't really understand his point when I first read the story.

That night in the open air, when I saw so many stars, I really wanted more than anything else to lean against Mother and count them. But I understood that it was impossible to count the stars. It was the first time I think I realized how vast the natural world is.

It was also the first time in my life that I had traveled so far. I already missed home. I felt so pitifully small . . . and so very sad.

I must above all work hard in order to succeed, so that Mother can at last have an easier life, can at last get rid of her pain and exhaustion. I hope that my wish comes true quickly and that Mother soon has a happier life.

Thursday, November 15
A fine day

This morning during gym we do a new kind of exercise: we go off to run in the streets instead of staying in the school yard.

Our class trails another class. We run as fast as we can to catch up with them and get ahead. By the time we do, I'm covered in sweat. The locals come out of their houses to watch us.

It's really great being a student. The only problem is that our parents suffer, especially my mother. If we don't work well, when our classroom is full of sunshine and our school full of joy, how will we ever be worth all the efforts our parents make on our behalf?

For the children of rich families, one day more or less makes no difference at all. For me, the child of a poor family, every day brings new trials with it. Not in terms of studying, because there I'm at the top of the class, but because of the kind of life we lead.

So I have to study hard without slacking in order not to suffer from hunger in the future.

Of course, the most important thing of all is my mother. I don't want her going so far away to work anymore. Our family will be happy, united. We'll have no more problems.

I haven't seen our politics teacher for several days. I'd like to see him very much, look at his face and hear his voice. His presence and his words always make me very happy. Somehow he offers consolation, relieving my sufferings and my problems. That's why I so want to see him come into the room. He has the ability to comfort anyone who is worried or unhappy.

I'm always full of suffering and worries. No sooner do I lower my head than Mother's words come into my mind, together with her ravaged hands. Why does this word *mother* leap into my mind so very often?

I like the politics teacher's way of using words as well as his manner. But I don't like the subject he teaches us. All we ever do is discuss heroes of history, patriotism, Taiwan, and morality. In each of his classes I secretly do my homework for other subjects. The teacher often says we should listen carefully. But I can't seem to correct my bad habits.

Today when we had a lesson with him, he picked me out, asked me to stand up. He wondered if I could answer a question. I shook my head. He let me sit down again. I know what he wanted to ask me: Could I listen more carefully during his class? That's why I refused to answer.

He shows me a lot of consideration, and I always disappoint him. From now on, I'm going to change my habits. I don't want to let him down anymore, or make him unhappy.

At noon after classes the comrades go home to eat. Since I'm a Hui, this is a fasting period for me. I've started Ramadan. This gives me a little free time.

In the street where I walk, I feel terribly alone. I think of Mother again. If only she were here . . . how wonderful that would be! Because everything I do is in relation to her.

If I make some kind of mistake, and haven't checked with her for her advice first, she chides me all day. Sometimes I resent her. But when I think about it, I know that she's doing it all for my own good. I mustn't get angry with her. If I hadn't followed her advice, where would I be today? I would lack maturity and I would understand nothing of the good things in life. If I hadn't had Mother teaching me, with all her criticisms, I wouldn't know what a fen or a yuan was, nor where they came from.

Without Mother, there would be no Ma Yan. I must be grateful to the woman who allowed her daughter to grow, to mature, and to become herself.

Thursday, November 22
A fine day

This week has flown by. It's already Thursday, and I don't know how we got here. I have a great wish to go home.

There's news in the village. We're putting in place measures that will allow the fields to be planted with trees. Each week when

151

I go home, the village has changed a little. The hills have acquired holes at regular intervals. In the spring we'll plant the trees. All of us will be really excited. Our land will turn green again.

I think that in a few years, or maybe a few decades, the landscape will have changed completely. These days, everywhere you look, there's only yellow earth. If you walk up to the high plateau to look down at the village, all you can see is yellow barrenness, a dried-out terrain. It's not even a landscape. To tell the truth, there's nothing to see.

Nor does the economy produce anything. Only *fa cai* allows one to live at all. The situation has to change. In the future, our village will be green. Its inhabitants will have acquired knowledge and will know how to build solid houses. If I work hard at school, when I grow up, I'll be able to devote my energy and skills to improving the cruel life of the villagers.

Wednesday, November 28
A bright day

This evening after classes a friend invited me home. She's like the little sister I would have liked to adopt. Her family lives fairly close to the school. There's only one valley to cross. On the way we meet several comrades who look happy. Seeing their joy, I too would like to be home. They all say how wonderful it is to sleep in one's own home.

At first when I get to my friend's house, I feel ill at ease. But her parents are very nice and ask me lots of questions. When we got there, her father came out onto the porch to welcome us. At my place when we have guests, it's my mother who welcomes them. Father stands near her, because he's not very savvy about dealing with people.

No sooner had we come in than my friend's parents brought us two bowls of meat. The steam was still rising from them. Then came fruit.

I envy my friend having a family that's so hospitable and happy. She doesn't have to worry about them. And they eat meat! I don't know how long it's been since we ate rice with meat at home. At the next market, I'd love to buy a little meat for Mother.

Tuesday, December 4
Light snow

Snow is floating in the air. I miss my village. We're in the midst of a history lesson, and the teacher goes on and on. I'm sitting near the window. When I turn my head, I can see snowflakes fluttering through the air before drifting to the ground. It takes me back to my childhood.

It was a very cold winter morning. Snow was falling thickly. My parents weren't home. They had gone far away to harvest *fa cai*.

My mother's illness started that winter. It was a hard and bitterly cold one. The snow rose high all around us, more snow than I had ever seen since I could remember. When the snow and wind stopped, my brothers, my grandmother (who was about seventy then), and I filled our underground tank with snow so that there would be no shortage of water during the winter.

Every Saturday when I'm at home, Mother asks me to collect up the donkey droppings. And I never manage it. She reminds me then of that snowbound winter. She says, "You were so little, but so brave. Now you've become weak and useless. What shall I do with you?"

Every time Mother talks like that, I remember the cold of that winter. I don't know how Mother and Father survived it. I don't know how I managed to carry all those bundles of snow. I don't really recall much except the cold and the snow. I only hope that I'm braver now than I was then.

Friday, December 7
A gray day

The fair is on today. My heart light, classes seemed to race past much more quickly than usual. I floated to the market, carried by one great hope. Last Saturday Mother promised she'd be there today. Since Ramadan is almost over, she has to come to the market to buy presents for people and invite an aged person home to break the fast.

The wind whistles, and it's so cold that you can't take your hands out of your pockets. As I walk through the streets I see all kinds of people shivering with cold. I look for Mother but I can't find her. The tears start to run down my face. They freeze into ice. I meet a lot of women wearing a white kerchief just like Mother's. I'm tempted to stop one of them, take her hand, call her "Mother" . . . but as soon as I step forward, I see that she isn't my mother and I stop myself.

I have the feeling someone is calling me. I turn around and see Father. My heart is suddenly less empty. But he isn't Mother. My father comes up to me, mutters a few words, and heads off. When it's Mother, she launches a barrage of questions at me. I love that. It's so engaging. And then it's so difficult to leave her.

Why do I spend so much time thinking about Mother?

Thursday, December 13
A fine day

It's market day again today. I'm very happy. I'm sure Mother will go and break the Ramadan fast with her maternal grandmother. But at the market, when I look for her, I can't find her. She hasn't come. The tears pour down my face. What a disappointment. Every market day I come in the hope of seeing her, and she isn't here. . . .

I'm walking with my head down when I see my maternal grandfather and my father. They're talking enthusiastically. But they're dressed in rags. Their clothes are dirty, their shoes full of holes. They look so ugly to me! On top of it all, they've got napkins around their waists, which makes them look even worse.

I don't know what my grandfather has eaten on this holy day, but as his granddaughter, I should be performing a pious act on his behalf. So I buy him fifty fen worth of apples, so that he can celebrate the end of the fast with them. But he disappears before I can give him his present.

At the vegetable market I meet my maternal grandmother. My grandfather asked her to buy some apples, she tells me. So I give her the apples I bought, and on top of it, go and buy pears for her. I've spent a great deal of money in very little time. It's not that I wanted to, but I couldn't do otherwise.

I turn back toward school. In front of the market entrance I see an old woman who reminds me of my paternal grandmother. I buy fifty fen of pears. She too looks over seventy; she's arrived at the age where one must have feelings of respect toward her.

I've used up all the money I intended to spend on a notebook. Apart from the thirty-five yuan I spent in the district capital when I went to take the entrance exams, this is the first time since elementary school that I've spent so much money all at once. Two yuan! But I had to. To honor a great feast day you have to buy good things to eat, beautiful clothes for the whole family. I have little enough apart from my sense of responsibility and the piety that lives in my heart.

Ma Yan with the first six schoolchildren funded by the readers of the newspaper *Libération*

WHAT HAPPENED NEXT

When the French newspaper *Libération* printed an extract from Ma Yan's diary in January 2002, readers responded in great numbers. They were touched by the fate of this Chinese girl, moved by her rebellion and her desperate desire to continue her schooling. Readers proposed financial help; some offered to finance her education, however long it took.

In response to this outpouring, we created a fund called the Association for the Children of Ningxia in the summer of 2002. This fund would help the children of families in need to continue their schooling. There was no question of creating a vast organization; we just wanted a simple system for sponsoring children. The only condition of the sponsorship was that the children wrote to us once a term to give us news of their studies and tell us how things were progressing.

After the publication of the article about Ma Yan, first twenty and then thirty children benefited from European sponsorship. This is a drop of water in an ocean of need, but it makes all the difference to these children. All of them wrote to us to say that school was going well.

The spontaneous gesture of Ma Yan's mother when she put the notebooks into our hands, a little like the way one tosses a message in a bottle to the high seas in desperate times, has had consequences far greater than she could have imagined. Her life, the life of her family, and the lives of many other children in this forgotten village at the end of the world have been transformed.

MA YAN'S LETTER

Dear Uncles and Aunts,*

How are you?** I received your letter on February 17, 2002. That day my father had gone to town for the market and he found the letter at the post office. He opened it right away, but there were a few characters he couldn't recognize. Back at home, he asked me to read it. When I had finished reading, I don't know why, but I broke out in a sweat, as if all my strength had gone. . . . Maybe it was because I was just too moved—too, too happy.

Father said, when he had finished reading the letter, that he no longer knew if he was walking on earth or in the sky, because he felt as if his body was floating. Mother added, "Finally, the heavens have opened their eyes. I didn't cry for no reason while I was up in the mountains. My tears then were the result of pain and sadness. Now they come from joy. I wish you a very good year and convey all my gratitude."

---

*In China, this is a respectful greeting from a child to adults. Ma Yan is writing to her sponsors.
**This phrase was written in English in the Chinese letter.

After reading your letter, I really understood what joy in this world means: friendship and the meaning of life. I thank all the people who have set out to help me. I am thrilled that young French people want to be my friends. I would like to write to them, phone them immediately, but I have neither their addresses nor phone numbers. Then too, they don't speak Chinese. I hope that you'll give them my address; I would like to be their friend, their best friend. I say "Thank you"* to all of them.

You said that you could help other children from families in need. I'm so very, very pleased about that. For me, my problems are now behind me. Let them, too, complete their schooling and fulfill their dreams. All my thanks.

Soon I'm going back to school. I will work very hard not to disappoint all your expectations.

I wish you great success in this Year of the Horse.

Ma Yan
February 19, 2002

---

*Also written in English.

HOW THINGS HAVE CHANGED

In Ma Yan's little house in the village of Zhangjiashu, a photo-graph of a class of French schoolchildren was hung with pride on the wall next to the family photographs. On the back of the photo the students had written, "Carry on with your schooling. French children are with you."

Pierre Haski and Ma Yan

As soon as the diary was published as a book, the responses started pouring in. A teacher in the east of France, whose pupils came from a particularly poor background and had real schooling difficulties, wrote to us to say that he regularly read the story of Ma Yan to his students, adding, "Some of them were genuinely touched by Ma Yan's story and expressed a desire to send her something or at least to try and correspond with her." What resulted were some twenty letters, drawings, and poems addressed to Ma Yan. Each of them had a ballpoint pen taped to it—a response to the diary entry in which she says she hadn't eaten so that she could buy a pen.

Dozens of letters from young French people, moved and indeed disturbed by Ma Yan's story, came to us, and through us went on to Ma Yan. The teenage magazine *L'Actu* voted Ma Yan "best-loved of the year 2002."

Indeed, the publication of Ma Yan's diary led to a great deal of support for the Association for the Children of Ningxia. The initial handful of members increased to three hundred by the end of the year. Donations allowed it to expand its work. At the beginning of the second school term in February 2003, the association gave out more grants, mostly to students at the middle school in Yuwang and the elementary school in Zhangjiashu. Children who would have had to leave school could now continue their education.

The association has also donated computers and purchased books to create a library at the Yuwang middle school. Additionally, the association has undertaken work to benefit the whole community and is exploring the possibility of digging a well in Zhangjiashu so that the villagers have clean water.

It is difficult to summarize the utter change in Ma Yan's life. A girl who never had enough to eat and seemed doomed to give up school and take up the miserable life of a village peasant is now a celebrity in Europe and to a certain extent in China as well. Thanks to the royalties from her book, she can eat her fill.

A Chinese magazine in December 2002 summed up the impact the book has had on its young heroine: "Ma Yan is happy, but stressed out!" Happy, most definitely, because she and her family have moved out of dire need, have proper winter clothes, and have bought some sheep and also a new television, which sits at the very center of the single room that is still their home. Happy, too, because she knows that the education she values so much is now secure for her. In 2004 she started high school in the city of Wuzhong, three hundred kilometers away from her home village. Ma Yan may attend a university too, if she works well—something that was almost unthinkable for a native of this impoverished village.

But she's also anxious, as the magazine said. First of all because in this village, like anywhere else in the world, success provokes jealousy and hostility. And also because Ma Yan has become a "model," an example to her comrades, which means she isn't allowed to make mistakes. On top of it all, she's had to assume a status that is challenging for a young peasant girl: it has involved being flown to Beijing to talk on national television. In March 2004 she was flown to Paris for a book fair, and there she was interviewed by media from around the world. The *New York Times* said of her diary, "Thanks to its publication, her family is no longer poor, and 250 Ningxia youngsters, mostly girls, now have scholarships to continue studying." The number of scholarships had grown to three hundred and fifty by the end of the year.

Chinese national television interviewed Ma Yan and her mother no less than three times, which gave her story extraordinary impact. Her diary, described as "legendary" by the Chinese media, is now published in China itself. Even Ma Yan's mother has begun to learn how to write.

But this courageous and intelligent young woman has taken on these changes with modesty and generosity. When we visited her in February 2003, she gave us a handwritten letter in which she made a solemn announcement:

I'm an ordinary pupil. I had help from certain friends. Today I want to offer love so that more poor students can enter into the world of knowledge through education. So that they can slowly make their dreams come true. So that they can build a better future for our country, our native land. If everyone offers up a little love, the world will be better. I want to give 25 percent of all my royalties from *The Diary of Ma Yan* to the Association for the Children of Ningxia.

Pierre Haski
Beijing, 2005

Ma Yan and her mother wave farewell.

Find out more about the Association for the
Children of Ningxia at its website:
www.enfantsduningxia.org

Or write to the association at:
Enfants du Ningxia
45, rue Notre-Dame de Nazareth
75003 Paris
France